the complete story of
the coachbuilders
Beccols & Bellhouse Hartwell
& how Blue Cars became
an important part of the tale

TWELVE ROYAL TIGERS

THIS PICTURE

Ready to go to the United States
and resplendent in the dark red livery
of St Christopher Travel Service of
New York with gold anodised trim,
the first of the Beccols-bodied Royal
Tigers for Blue Cars is inspected by
Blue Cars director Robert Langton,
brother of Ted Langton, and publicity
manager T G Davies.

NICHOLS ARCHIVE
colour work by Michael Eyre

FRONT COVER

The coach that never was.
The original plan was that all 12 of
Blue Cars' Royal Tigers should have
this style of body, the first finished in
the maroon livery of St Christopher
Travel Service, New York, for the tour
of the USA and Canada, and the
others in Blue Cars' attractive blue.
In the event there were no blue ones
of this style. This coloured image
shows what one would have
looked like.

NICHOLS ARCHIVE
colour work by Michael Eyre,
Ray Stenning & Paul Fitchie

BACK COVER

The coaches that replaced them.
One of Blue Cars' first six Bellhouse
Hartwell Landmasters.

BELLHOUSE HARTWELL ARCHIVE
colour work by Michael Eyre,
Ray Stenning & Paul Fitchie

told by

Michael Eyre · **Peter Greaves** · **Martin Ingle**
Michael Fenton · **Chris Howard**

with additional research by

John Bennett · **John Kaye** · **Peter Tulloch**

designed by **Ray Stenning of Best Impressions**
printed by **Lavenham Press**
published by **Best Impressions 15 Starfield Road London W12 9SN**
copyright © **D M Eyre for and on behalf of the authors 2012**

a superb Classic Bus production

ISBN 978 0 9565740 2 2

Introduction

For many years coachbuilding firms were plentiful in the north west of England. First amongst these was the mighty Leyland Motors which, although its main business was the manufacture of truck and passenger chassis, had a substantial body shop. Others were major names in bus or coach bodywork - East Lancashire Coachbuilders Ltd in Blackburn, the Northern Counties Motor and Engineering Co Ltd in Wigan, H V Burlingham Ltd in Blackpool and Crossley Motors Ltd in Manchester and Stockport. .

Then came well-known mid-sized firms such as Massey Brothers of Wigan. Also from that town was Santus Motor Body Works Ltd, which made some 500 coach bodies; and Pearson's Ltd of Liverpool and Trans-United Coach-craft Ltd in Rochdale each produced around 240. Most of the small firms were jobbing coachbuilders, mainly making van and lorry bodies but building a few coach bodies particularly when demand was at a peak after the ending of the 1939-1945 war - examples are County Motors (Leigh) Ltd, KW Bodies Ltd of Blackpool, Stockport Manufacturing Co Ltd, Stockport, and Universal Coachworks Ltd of Oldham.

Two of the mid-sized firms had a particularly interesting life. Bellhouse, Hartwell & Co Ltd was based in Daisy Hill, Westhoughton, about halfway between Bolton and Wigan. It built some 275 coach bodies. A mile or so closer to Bolton in Chequerbent (not to be confused with Chowbent which was the local name for nearby Atherton) was the modest works of Beccols Ltd which built 124. Their stories are interlinked - two senior members of the Bellhouse firm left to form Beccols in 1946. In 1950 and 1951 both firms would become involved in the supply of 12 Leyland Royal Tiger coaches to the up-market continental travel business of Blue Cars (Continental) Ltd and Beccols would go bankrupt as a result, Bellhouse Hartwell would move into the aircraft industry and Blue Cars' owner would go on to establish Britannia Airways.

This is a tale of entrepreneurship, design, style and pioneering, which, by the nature of such things, involves failure as well as success. However, the story has a happy ending - every one of the principal players found success in his own way.

Most of the images in the book are black and white - the principal events took place before colour photography of coaches became commonplace.

Acknowledgments

We have had generous encouragement and support from the families of the founders of the firms involved, who were keen to see the story written.

Kim Kynaston *grandson of Fred Bellhouse*
Penny Fletcher *née Hartwell, daughter of Alec Hartwell*
Rupert Fletcher *grandson of Alec Hartwell*
the late George Nichols
the late Winifred Nichols *widow of Brian Nichols*
Dorothy née Beckett *daughter of Bert Beckett*
Roy Smirk *friend and colleague of Bert Beckett*
June Mead *daughter of Blue Cars founder Ted Langton*

Many of the images in this book are from their private collections - in the case of the two coachbuilding firms, these are acknowledged to either the Bellhouse Hartwell archive or the Nichols archive. Bellhouse Hartwell staff members:

Fred and Marion Taylor
Alan Lee
Harry Foster
John Morrison
George Martin
provided memories and records.

We have had help from many transport historians, including:
David Gray
Bob Hobbs
Cyril McIntyre
Bob Smith
Ken Swallow

together with valuable contributions from
The Omnibus Society
The PSV Circle
The Kithead Trust
The NA3T Photographic Archive
The J S Cockshott Archive
The Bolton Evening News
The London Gazette
The Travel Trade Gazette
the staff of the Companies House Archives, Cardiff

Any errors, however, are due to the authors. We have endeavoured to identify the photographers and apologise if any are wrongly attributed.

Contents

Below is the Beccols Roadmaster, a version of which for Smith's of Wigan caused Blue Cars to contact Beccols. This picture, however, is of Crossley's demonstrator, which subsequently became JWW 676.

CROSSLEY MOTORS

chapter 1

Bellhouse Higson

At the entrance to the works road was Greenvale House, where Alec Hartwell lived for many years.

BELLHOUSE HARTWELL ARCHIVE

The story starts in the Lancashire cotton industry. In July 1914 William Higson of Leigh and James Shuttleworth of Tyldesley formed William Higson and Co Ltd to expand their existing cotton doubling, reeling and winding business. They had previously been in partnership and the new firm, which had a capital of £1,000 in £1 shares, continued to be based at Smallbrook Mill, Westleigh, Leigh.

By mid-1915 the firm was short of cash, needing £700 to pay for plant and motor vehicles, which it had leased or rented from the South Lancashire Tramways Co. This sizeable sum (a high quality motor car cost £400 in those days) was beyond the means of the founders. It was provided in August 1915 by 24 year-old Charles Frederick (Fred) Bellhouse who raised a mortgage to cover this and other items. Already a member of the Manchester Cotton Exchange, he had offices in the city and lived in Prestwich. As a condition Bellhouse became Governing Director, Higson and Shuttleworth losing their voting power and control. The position was consolidated one year later when Bellhouse received shares in settlement of any and all other debts.

In June 1925 the firm's name was changed to Bellhouse, Higson and Company Limited (Bellhouse Higson) with Higson and Bellhouse as directors, Fred Bellhouse remaining controlling director. The company expanded, first into bleaching and dyeing and then in a very different direction.

Alec Hartwell, Fred Bellhouse's nephew, was born in 1914 in Chorlton, Manchester; his mother was the sister of Fred Bellhouse's wife, Dorothy, and the two families had lived close to each other. Alec had not long started at William Hulme's Grammar School, Manchester when an accident to his father forced him to leave and to take over his father's agency selling baby carriages. This he did with the flair and success which would characterise his business life. Although only 15 he taught himself to drive and quickly doubled the sales. His main interest, however, was motor vehicles and he spent all his spare time helping a neighbour tinkering with car engines. A contemporary newspaper cartoon featured a character called *Jim the Mechanic* and his family began to call him this as a joke. The nickname Jim stuck and most of his work colleagues and staff knew him as Jim Hartwell, although we use the name Alec in this book. Recognising his nephew's potential, in 1934 Fred Bellhouse recruited Alec, buying a new £100 Ford car to enable him to get from Chorlton to the works in Leigh.

The firm suffered a disastrous fire in June 1935 when Smallbrook Mill was destroyed. The Manchester-based Bleachers Association Ltd came to the rescue, leasing the firm the unused Association-owned Greenvale Print & Dye Works in Leigh Road, Daisy Hill, Westhoughton.

An interest in things mechanical and technological innovation was to become Alec Hartwell's lifelong passion and had great influence on the company. He always wanted to be first into any new ground-breaking project or idea - anything that was old or 'not the latest' did not interest him. During the late 1930s he took flying lessons at Barton Aerodrome and gained his private pilot's licence. Much later he would fly in his own plane each week from Leavesden, near Watford, close to his then house at Penn, Buckinghamshire, to Manchester en route to his businesses in Burnley. In addition to flying, which he only gave up when aged 77, his other interests were fast yachts and motor boats (including racing a yacht and a hydroplane on Windermere) and photography.

As with many technologists, these speed- and technology-based interests were linked with a mercurial, impatient temperament, intolerant of those, including his family and his uncle, who seemed to him not to 'keep up'. Thus he was not the easiest of people with whom to work or live - one kindly-said quote was, *". . . and that's putting it politely"* - but successful he surely was.

During the 1930s the Lancashire textile industry was hit hard by the depression and the growing import of cotton goods. Bellhouse Higson's business was no exception. Alec persuaded his uncle that the cotton trade would never recover and that they should diversify into engineering. The first move was into making aluminium pots and pans and to take charge of this activity he recruited Cuthbert (Bert) Beckett, a skilled sheet metal worker and panel beater from motor dealer Simister's of Bolton.

Alec Hartwell had wider plans and was soon suggesting building bodies for luxury coaches. Magazine accounts claim that a small number of prototype coach bodies were built and tested in 1938. The only one traced was built on an early Leyland Tiger chassis for the Ardwick, Manchester coach firm of J. Simpson who lived close to Alec Hartwell. It is possible that another may have been taken by the government for the war effort.

Although press reports indicated that Bellhouse Higson built several prototype bodies, there is only a picture of this one - shown below in grey primer outside Greenvale works, with another coach chassis in the foreground. Built for J Simpson of Ardwick, Manchester, a friend of Alec Hartwell, the coach's identity is not visible but it is fairly certain that it was FV 1902, a Leyland TS3. New in 1931 with a Burlingham body, it had several owners before being acquired by Simpson. It ran with its new body, again with several owners, until 1953.

Alec Hartwell had wanted to copy Harrington's dorsal fin style, shown in the lower picture, but it was protected by a patent.

BELLHOUSE HARTWELL ARCHIVE

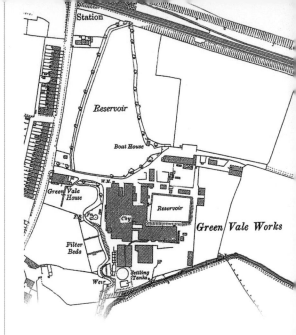

Above is a map of Greenvale Works in 1928. Daisy Hill railway station is at the top of the map. Based on the 1928 Ordnance Survey map.

CROWN COPYRIGHT RESERVED

Below is Greenvale Works from the air in the 1960s, aligned in accordance with the map above. The curved roof building was erected after the war and housed coach assembly.

BELLHOUSE HARTWELL ARCHIVE

5

It was Fred Bellhouse's faith in the abilities of his young nephew that led to the success of Bellhouse Hartwell.

This is Fred and his wife Dorothy with a Vauxhall Velox at their Prestwich home in the 1950s - their own family was three daughters.

BELLHOUSE HARTWELL ARCHIVE

In addition to aircraft parts, Bellhouse Higson also built 50 of these mobile canteen bodies on Fordson 7Y chassis for the NAAFI.

BELLHOUSE HARTWELL ARCHIVE

For the coach's design he wanted to copy Harrington's dorsal fin design but was unable to do so because Harrington had patented it. However, the first coach bodies were to a design which owed something to this.

Work on coach bodies was halted by the preparations for war. Having a private pilot's licence, when war was declared Alec Hartwell applied to join the RAF as a pilot. The government decided that he would be more useful to the war effort in an expansion of the Bellhouse Higson sheet metal business. His application was refused and one can be reasonably certain that the civil servant responsible was on the receiving end of some very forthright views from Alec Hartwell.

Nevertheless, the decision was a good one for the country and the business. The sheet metal workshop was soon busy making wing tips, fins, rudders and pilot's seats for Spitfires, Lancasters and other aircraft. It quickly expanded to complex aircraft parts such as drop fuel tanks and developed a close working relationship with Manchester-based AV Roe and Co Ltd which would continue for many years after the war. Wishing to further the vehicle building ambitions, in 1941/42 the firm also obtained a government contract for 50 timber-framed mobile canteen bodies on Fordson 7Y chassis for the NAAFI.

Extra skills were needed and 42 year-old George Nichols joined the firm. Born in Buckinghamshire in 1901, he served an apprenticeship at Wolverton railway workshops, becoming a skilled coachbuilder. During the First World War he enlisted in the Royal Flying Corps and afterwards went to work in the motor car body business with Daimler. He moved north when he met his wife, joining Liverpool motor dealer and coachbuilder J Blake and Co. In 1928 he moved to Wigan bus body builder Northern Counties, rising from charge hand, to foreman and finally Works Manager. He also lectured on coachbuilding at evening classes at Wigan Technical College.

In 1940 because of the war, almost all United Kingdom bus building was halted for a year or so and Northern Counties was directed to assemble American military trucks for which George Nichols set up and ran a successful production line. Sadly the rigours of long hours seven days a week affected his health and on doctor's

advice he was forced to look for a less demanding post. Alec Hartwell quickly recruited him as foreman of one of the assembly shops, in a parallel role to Bert Beckett. Staff numbers at Greenvale grew to 700 with the textile business restricted to the first floor of the works.

With the prospect of an end to the war and Nichols and Beckett on board, Alec Hartwell made plans to build more coach bodies. The government authorised coach production on a limited scale from March 1946 but materials for such work remained under government allocation, priority being given to bus bodies. However, the firm probably had sufficient aluminium and other materials left from its war work to make a start and may also have had some parts from uncompleted pre-war coach bodies in store. There was a huge pent up demand for both new coaches and for new bodies on pre-war chassis returned from military duties. Greenvale completed its first in 1946, it being licensed in January 1947.

The plan had been disrupted in mid-1946 by the departure of Bert Beckett and George Nichols to start their own coachbuilding firm. The Beccols founders'

Alec Hartwell always wanted to be first into any new ground-breaking project or idea - anything that was old or 'not the latest' did not interest him.

In 1947 the body on his Alvis 4.3-litre car, shown at the bottom, looked dated, and the works rebuilt it to a more streamlined style, shown in the upper picture. Anyone familiar with coachbuilding will admire the panel work.

BELLHOUSE HARTWELL ARCHIVE

families assert that the departure was simply because, *"they wanted to run their own company and do their own thing"* but the actual events are lost in the mists of time. Being by then aged around 45, they may have found it difficult working for the younger, mercurial Alec - some of the staff certainly did and there were frequent if short strikes in the late 1940s.

Also, whilst still working for Bellhouse Higson, Beckett and Nichols had been doing some body construction at weekends on their own account to raise cash for their intended new business, renting a shed in Over Hulton where they built at least one caravan. There is little doubt that this put them in a conflict of interest situation and if Alec Hartwell had discovered what they were doing, there seems little doubt that he would have fired them on the spot.

Whatever the real cause, Bert Beckett and George Nichols left and on 23rd July 1946 registered their own firm, Beccols Ltd, based in Chequerbent and only a mile or so from Daisy Hill. The Beccols name was derived from syllables of the surnames of the two founders.

chapter 2

Beccols gets started

Beccols stated business objective was to build coaches and commercial vehicles bodies. The date of formation was nicely timed to take orders for deliveries for the 1947 coaching season.

The founders had already found a site in Norris Road, Chequerbent, Westhoughton - a short unadopted road off the north-east side of the A6 just east of the junction of Park Road and the A6 (Manchester Road) at the side of the Bolton - Kenyon Junction railway line. Passing Chequerbent Station the road led to and was named after the modestly sized Norris Steel Works; also adjacent was a scrap metal merchant Joseph Holt. The area and road layout was much changed by the construction of the M6 motorway but Norris Road and the (empty) Beccols site still existed at the time of writing.

Materials for new buildings were impossible to obtain and the partners bought four surplus semicircular-roofed Nissen-style buildings from the government and erected them on the site themselves. The section which was high enough to accommodate a coach was narrow and each hut was only some 150ft long so that when the firm was busy, *"we had to do finishing work outside in the road in the open air because there was no room inside"*. With a steelworks and scrapyard across the road and passing steam trains, it was not ideal.

One building was the body shop, where the bodies were built and panelled, the next was the trim shop, then the paint shop and finally a blacksmiths' and metalworking shop. Also within the huts were the woodworking, metal-forming and other machines, stores, office and the like. Machinery was in short supply but the founders were able to acquire sufficient at sales and auctions. The curved roof meant that coaches could only fit in the centre of the huts and even then the fit could be described as snug. By contrast, working conditions were not. The huts were, *"very cold, there was no heating apart from one pot-bellied stove in each hut - it was freezing in winter"*.

George Nichols looked after the design and drawings whilst Bert Beckett was in charge of sales, construction and general management; both were involved in hands-on vehicle building. The first coach bodies were finished in August 1947, by which time Bellhouse Hartwell had delivered twelve. Unsurprisingly, Beccols' design was similar to that of Bellhouse Hartwell. Later Beccols bodies showed more of George Nichols' bold design ideas - for example, the firm was early into cantilevered front ends on fully-fronted coaches.

Beccols' works was just off the A6 in Norris Road, Chequerbent - a short unadopted track which led to and was named after the modestly sized Norris Steel Works; the other company in the road was Joseph Holt, a scrap metal merchant.

Beckett and Nichols bought four surplus 'Nissen' huts, similar to those shown below, from the War Department and put them up themselves. Machinery was also in short supply but the founders were able to acquire sufficient basic equipment at sales and auctions.

NICHOLS ARCHIVE

It took some time to get orders for coaches and commercial vehicle bodies, and even then there was a wait for new or reconditioned pre-war chassis. The early gaps in the workload were filled by a variety of jobs including repair of an Austin limousine, a furniture van body, a showman's caravan and some refurbishing work on motor cars. One developed into the regular supply of bodies for the Jowett 'Bradford' vans sold by local dealer Boydell of Horwich; later the partners each bought a Jowett Javelin car from the firm.

The first coach job was the rebuild of a Leyland Tiger for Progress of Chorley. George's son remembered working night and day on the job - *"It was booked to go to a match at Wembley and it did - although it was only in primer paint"*. The first new coach bodies were for James Smith & Co (Wigan) Ltd (Smith's), which was owned by Webster Brothers (Wigan) Ltd. Smith's bought from both Beccols and Bellhouse Hartwell, probably to obtain early delivery but possibly also due to local friendly connections.

Ownership of the firm was 50/50 Beckett and Nichols but it seems that Bert Beckett provided the greater share of funds (*"although he never told his wife that this was so"*); there was no other financial backing. The founders built up a good business, eventually employing 80 to 100 people. The bodies perhaps did not have the exceptional quality or detail finish of Bellhouse Hartwell's but they lasted well and had proper northern values - a good, stylish job at a fair price.

The huts were narrow and only some 150ft in length such that when the firm was busy "we had to do finishing work outside in the road in the open air because there was no room inside". The huts were "very cold, there was no heating apart from one pot-bellied stove in each hut - it was freezing in winter".

The curved roof meant that coaches could only fit down their centre and even then the fit could be described as "snug". It says much for the staff that they could produce a good finish in such cramped space. Nichols archive

NICHOLS ARCHIVE

Completed in August 1947, Beccols'
first coach was a Leyland Tiger PS1
for Smith's of Wigan.

In the picture below George Nichols
(left), Bert Beckett (centre) and Fred
Webster, manager of Webster Bros,
which owned Smith's, stand proudly
with the newly completed coach,
against a background of the
steelworks.

NICHOLS ARCHIVE

Initially, Bellhouse Hartwell and Beccols focussed on customers in the North West. However, whilst Bellhouse Hartwell took early steps to widen its coach market and also to diversify into aerospace work and sheet metal products, Beccols' sales were mainly to smaller coach operators. There was nothing wrong with this - the firm was smaller than Bellhouse Hartwell and the North West was a good market with strong local associations where 'grape vines' and 'old boy networks' could be relied upon to ensure a fair deal and prompt payment.

Beccols' initial coach body was similar to Bellhouse Hartwell's, having a rounded, turned under back end. Like Bellhouse Hartwell later in 1948 this was updated ready for the 1949 season deliveries with a more up to date rear with the rear mudguard trim taken round the back end. The three large strips of broad polished aluminium moulding became something of a Beccols feature.

Unlike Bellhouse Hartwell, Beccols was always willing to do 'specials' or something different. In 1948/9 Beccols bodied fourteen Commer normal-control (engine in front of driver) chassis which had started life during the war as government lorries. Sold in 1947/8 as government surplus, many were bought by dealers, refurbished and fitted with coach bodies. The Beccols ones were almost certainly for one or other of such dealers and as a result were sold to operators much further afield than Beccols' normal market. By contrast, two 1948 Commer Commandos, in spite of their military-sounding name, were new post-war coach chassis bodied for Beccols' usual market - late in 1948 the Rootes Group replaced the Commando with the forward-control Avenger and this prompted the conversion of the wartime lorries.

In 1949 two lightweight Austin normal-control chassis received the first Beccols Roadmaster full-front coach bodies, having first been converted to forward-control. Covered in later chapters of this book, the Roadmaster is an important part of the Beccols story.

Beccols also developed its commercial vehicle body business, in particular building tipper bodies for the substantial Bolton-based vehicle builder Bromilow and Edwards Ltd (B&E). The limited size of the Nissen huts meant that the latter were built 'off chassis' and taken to B&E's Bolton works for fitting. Another lucrative, if smallish activity was building the highly polished and decorated living vans used by showmen. Both were a good way of levelling out the seasonal demand for coaches - operators wanted their new vehicles at the start of each season and work tended to tail off after July.

Although the country-wide demand for new coaches would drop very considerably in 1950 causing many small coachbuilders to close down, it is likely that with its commercial work for Bromilow and Edwards, Beccols could have continued for several more years as a 'jobbing coachbuilder' willing and able to do specials and one-offs. The firm's weakness was its financial resources. Beccols would find this out in a particularly harsh way but before that unhappy part of the story, it is necessary to follow the rising fortunes of Alec Hartwell down the road at Greenvale.

The interior of the coach was nicely finished with a cheerful flower-pattern moquette for the seats.

NICHOLS ARCHIVE

Coachwork
by Beccols

One of the first Beccols coach bodies was completed in mid-1947. Intended for Pownall of Golborne, it was supplied by dealer Frank Ellison (Warrington) Ltd.

Use of the Thornycroft Nippy lorry chassis for a coach led to problems with its tilt test. Changes were made to the rear axle and wheels and after that it was taken by Pownall.

In 1949 it passed to Thomson of Kirkwall in Orkney, where it had a long life running as a bus until 1957, latterly with Nicolson of Kirkwall. It then spent a further eight years as a mobile shop.

This picture was taken across the road from Ellison's premises at 447 Manchester Road, Warrington. Ellison's via John Shearman

ELLISON'S via JOHN SHEARMAN

Beccols bodied 14 normal-control Commer Q4 chassis which had started life as wartime government lorries. Sold to dealers as government surplus in 1947/8, some 400 Q4s were fitted with new coach bodies.

Beccols' 14 were for one or other of the several dealers that did such conversions, and were therefore sold on to a much wider market than Beccols normally covered. DHJ 397 went to Cox of Southend - the firm was taken over by Cook, Westcliff with whom it is pictured on the Southend seafront.

MIKE FENTON

After the war, the first priority for passenger chassis deliveries was for buses; coaches came second. Coach building was also fairly seasonal, most operators wanting new coaches ready for the start of the season at Easter.

To fill the gaps in work on coaches, Beccols built timber commercial vehicle bodies, mainly under sub-contract to the Bolton firm of Bromilow and Edwards, which made the Edbro system for tipper trucks, and some of Beccols' work was done at the latter's premises in Bolton.

The upper two on this page are Austins and one below is a Leyland Beaver, all photographed outside the Bromilow and Edwards works in Bolton.

NICHOLS ARCHIVE

On this page are three more examples of Beccols' commercial bodies. Many were for the Manchester Austin dealer, Syd Abrams Ltd - who, many years on, would acquire what remained of the successors to the Beccols business.

The ice cream van was on a battery-powered Morrison Electricar chassis.

These views of JOM 800, a Crossley SD42/7 new in
May 1949 for Jackson of Ward End, Castle Bromwich,
Birmingham, show the revised rear end design.
The three strips of aluminium trim on the rear wing
valence were something of a Beccols trademark.
The result still looked heavy.

Beccols early publicity, as shown on the right,
was relatively modest.

NICHOLS ARCHIVE

33 SEATER LUXURY COACH

By **BECCOLS LTD.**   Chequerbent, Bolton, Lancashire

Phone : Westhoughton 2222   Grams : Coachwork, Westhoughton

Beccols' first body on a Foden was on a Gardner 5LW-engined PVSC5 chassis for the well-known local operator John Monks and Sons Ltd of Leigh. Foden's impressive engine cowl enhanced any design. JTB 20 was licenced in December 1947.

Wigan, St Helens and Leigh are rugby towns and this view, with several others in this book, was taken by Arthur Hustwitt when the coaches were at Wembley for Rugby League Cup Finals.

NA3T/A HUSTWITT COLLECTION

Monks bought a second Beccols-bodied Foden in 1949, KTD 877, which had a Gardner 5LW engine. The coach was later rebuilt with a full-width front; its engine was quickly changed to a 6LW.

Another later alteration was the odd-looking wrap-around glazed back end, which looks more like the work of KW Bodies of Bispham. Beccols was always willing to do specials but does not seem to have done this particular rebuild.

Here it is at the 1954 Rugby League Cup Final with the twin towers of the old Wembley stadium as backdrop. The match, Halifax v Warrington was a draw and was replayed at Odsal, Bradford, a couple of weeks later. Appropriately for a book about Lancashire firms and people, the replay result was Warrington 8 Halifax 4.

NA3T/A HUSTWITT COLLECTION

THE RUGBY LEAGUE CHALLENGE CUP COMPETITION

FINAL TIE
HALIFAX
v
WARRINGTON
SATURDAY, APRIL 24th, 1954   KICK-OFF 3 pm

EMPIRE STADIUM
WEMBLEY
OFFICIAL PROGRAMME   ONE SHILLING

chapter 3

Growth at Greenvale

Alec Hartwell quickly hired replacements for his departed managers. Perhaps catalysed by their loss but more likely a result of his wish to have ownership of what he had created, on 22nd January 1947 Bellhouse, Hartwell and Company Limited (Bellhouse Hartwell) was registered and Bellhouse Higson's sheet metal business, including coachbuilding, was transferred to it.

Fred Bellhouse and Alec Hartwell each owned 50% of the shares. Alec was general manager and he and his family lived for many years in the substantial Greenvale House situated at the front of the Greenvale site. In 1948 the works was expanded with the addition of a substantial arc-roofed building in which the coaches were then assembled. Bellhouse Higson's textile activities continued on the first floor of the main works, trading successfully and profitably into the 1960s - for example supplying sewing cotton to tailors Burton's and the Woolworth's store chain.

Whilst interested in all things new and technical, Alec Hartwell was also an astute, tough business manager. For example, he would not release a completed coach until he not only had the cheque for the full amount but also had his financial staff phone the client's bank to confirm that there were sufficient available funds to honour it - and would keep the client talking in his office whilst this was done. On another occasion, there was a delay in Greenvale delivering cockpit fairings for the AVRO 748 aircraft and, having over-ordered, AVRO wrote to cancel the order. On the day the cancellation letter dropped through the letterbox at Greenvale, Bellhouse Hartwell's lorry arrived at AVRO's works loaded with the balance of the order - and the invoice.

With a pronounced rounded and turned under back, the first coach bodies were based on the pre-war design and around five seem to have incorporated parts made for bodies started but not completed before the war. A few of the early post-war bodies carried Bellhouse Higson transfers and are recorded as such in some lists. So far as we have been able to determine, only two post-war bodies were completed before Bellhouse Hartwell was formed and it was probably a case of using up maker's transfers with the Higson name on them which were already in stock whilst awaiting delivery of the Bellhouse Hartwell version.

An updated style with a more modern rear end was produced for the 1948 season. A feature of the bodies was that there was a large proportion of steel framing - the vertical pillars for example. Use of steel pillars was not uncommon amongst the large coachbuilders but rare in small firms. The quality of build, trimming, detailing and general finish was very high and this quality would be a feature of anything that Bellhouse Hartwell made - from pots and pans, through coach bodies to sub-assemblies for jet airliners.

Like Beccols, to smooth out the seasonal demand for coach deliveries, it did build a large number of timber tipper bodies under sub-contract from Bromilow and Edwards Ltd, which held a major patent on hydraulic tipping gear and owned tipper makers Edbro and Pilot. There was a brief excursion into fire tender bodywork but

The first few bodies carried Bellhouse Higson maker's transfers although, strictly, all except the first two were finished after Bellhouse, Hartwell & Co Ltd had been formed.

Four were delivered between January and May 1947, to Smith's / Webster of Wigan, three on pre-war Leyland chassis acquired from the War Department which had requisitioned them in 1940, and the fourth on a new Leyland PS1.

AG 8280, at the bottom of the opposite page, was a Leyland TS4 new in 1932 to Western SMT. The bulbous turned-under rear did little to enhance the coach's looks; it also had the pre-war style of passenger door.

BELLHOUSE HARTWELL ARCHIVE

At the top of the opposite page KJ 5433 was another 1932 Leyland TS4, new to Maidstone & District. It was still in good order when with a showman in September 1962 - evidence of build quality.

Above, Leyland Tiger TS6 CK 4748 was new to Ribble in 1933. Rebodied in 1948 it had the revised rear end and looked much more up to date. It later passed to Benson of Accrington, with whom it is in this June 1958 picture.

J S COCKSHOTT ARCHIVE

KKC 41, a Foden PVSC6 for Topping's Super Coaches of Liverpool, featured in the Bellhouse Hartwell 1949 advertisement above.

A full-front version of the standard body was built on a Foden for Rigby of Patricroft. Registered LTD 536, it was new in 1950.

BELLHOUSE HARTWELL ARCHIVE

only two were made for the Bolton brigade. The firm also built some showman's caravans principally for the Sedgwick family of showmen, including a very costly one for the head of the family. Built on an Austin chassis, the luxurious body was panelled inside in specially-imported expensive Japanese Maple.

In coach bodies, however, Bellhouse Hartwell built one design exclusively on forward-control heavyweight chassis and did not follow Beccols' path into specials or normal-control lightweight chassis. The rounded rear end having been changed to something more modern, the only subsequent variation was the deletion of the small valence panel in front of the door and a rearrangement of the decorative trim on the sides of the coach. The only chassis exceptions during this period were five normal-control Leyland Comets and a single Commer Avenger.

The hollowware business was very profitable and it, too, expanded, using the brand name Belso. By 1951 pots, pans, butter coolers, tea and coffee sets, and the like were being produced, with large contracts for major clients such as Woolworth's, then a household name. These, too, were of high quality and very durable - the authors discovered one family which was still using its set of Belso Ware pans in 2010. Other Belso products were a range of children's pedal cars, step ladders and motor car and coach wheel trims.

The Belso range was sold to wholesalers and large customers. Fred Bellhouse looked after their sales and the textile work and most Belso sales were in the name of Bellhouse Higson. Although manufacture remained at Greenvale, sales and marketing used the Bellhouse's Whitefield home address - Alec Hartwell was in charge at Greenvale.

His interest in flying and anything up-to-date undiminished, Alec Hartwell developed the links with the aircraft industry - there was a rising demand for high quality accurate sheet-metal based work for what was becoming known as the aerospace industry. Staff numbers rose to over 200.

Coachwork
by Bellhouse Hartwell

The photograph on this page and the two on the next page were taken on the entrance road to Greenvale works. These pictures show what became the standard Bellhouse Hartwell half-cab coach body.

HARTWELL ARCHIVE

VH 5730, above, was an AEC Regent new in 1933 to Huddersfield Corporation. After the Second World War it passed to Wright of Bootle, which had Bellhouse Hartwell rebody it as a coach. It had been sold to Mowbray (Diamond) of Stanley in County Durham when this picture was taken in July 1958.

J S COCKSHOTT ARCHIVE

Wright of Newark had KVO 127, the AEC Regal shown in the upper picture on the left, in 1949. It had revised side decoration of polished aluminium strip instead of the painted flash, which was beginning to look somewhat 'pre-war'.

ROY MARSHALL

Edwin Holden of Oldham was a regular Bellhouse Hartwell client, buying four AEC Regals (EBU 495-98) and four Leyland Tiger PS1s (EBU 494, 790, 816/17) in 1948 for his companies - Stanley Spencer's Tours Ltd and Tom Shaw & Son (Greenfield) Ltd.

HARTWELL ARCHIVE

At the top is Leyland Comet LTD 787, still with its original owner, Ireland of Lancaster, in August 1963. In this picture it is leaving Bradford having been on hire to Ribble for a Yorkshire Pool service.

J S COCKSHOTT ARCHIVE

At the end of 1949 Smith's of Wigan bought new bodies for two of its pre-war Leyland Tigers - JP 1570 and JP 1689 - shown in the upper picture on the right.

OMNIBUS SOCIETY

FNV 541, in the bottom picture on the right, was an Albion Valiant for Basford of Greens Norton, Northants.

ROY MARSHALL

New May 1950, LKB 525 on the left was a Commer Avenger for Topping's Super Coaches of Liverpool. It was the only body that Bellhouse Hartwell built on a lightweight chassis until the Fordsons.

BELLHOUSE HARTWELL ARCHIVE

New to Jones of Ruabon, Foden GCA 54, in the colour picture above, passed to Strachan's Deeside Omnibuses of Ballater in 1959. It ran for them until May 1965 when the firm was sold to Alexander Northern, which sold the coach to a dealer in December 1965.

IAIN MACGREGOR

Guy Arab FAW 787, on the left, was one of a pair for Vagg of Knockin Heath, Shropshire, who also had two Bellhouse-bodied Crossley SD42s.

ROY MARSHALL

chapter 4
A complete range

Alec Hartwell had wider ambitions for his coachbuilding business, aiming to become a major player in the industry, offering a complete range of coach bodies and once the half-cab range was established in production his thoughts turned to a full range of standard bodies. That he could afford to do all this was due to the success of the other activities at Greenvale.

In doing so, it was always unlikely that he would stick to middle-of-the-road coach designs and in 1949 Bellhouse Hartwell produced something avant garde and unusual.

The Transatlantic - soon shortened to Atlantic - was innovative and ingenious. The aim was to achieve maximum seating capacity on a forward-engined chassis, with a virtually flat floor throughout the coach and all seats at the same level. It could accommodate 39 passengers on a 27ft 6in chassis, which would normally carry 33 or 35 at most. This was made possible by the introduction of the Foden PVFE6 chassis with its front-mounted Foden two-stroke engine which was of much lower overall height than a normal four-stroke unit and set low in the chassis. With some ingenuity it was possible to build the coach's floor flat with a small hump over the engine and a corresponding (and very noticeable) one in the roof. Bellhouse Hartwell was granted a patent for the design in 1949 and then offered it to the general industry by means of a licence payment. It was licensed to Heaver (which built two) and Whitson (none).

Whilst the result was a practical vehicle, it is hard to deny that the design, influenced by American styling, looked ugly and unfashionable to British eyes. Also, the Atlantic could only be built on the Foden chassis and two-stroke engines were something that did not appeal to the British market. The final nail in the Atlantic's coffin was the acceptance of the 30ft-long underfloor-engined chassis which more or less ended the market for heavyweight forward-engined coach chassis overnight. However, in 1949 it was by no means certain that, in spite of operator pressure, the government would permit 30ft-long coaches, which it did without much warning in June 1950 (a few weeks later the restriction on the general use of 8ft-wide buses and coaches was removed equally suddenly), or that the generally conservative British bus and coach operators would turn so quickly to underfloor-engined chassis.

The second member of the range was a Ford-based version of the popular 29-seat Bedford OB with Duple Vista body. Once again the concept was innovative and the design bold and striking. Although there was a continuing demand for a 29-seater, Bedford had decided to end production of the OB and replace it with the 33-seat 27-ft Bedford SB/Duple Vega. Bedford and Duple dominated that segment of the market and the idea of a Ford alternative looked attractive.

The chassis was the new normal-control Fordson ET (ET meant nothing more 'European Truck'), which had been introduced in 1949. Ford was renaming its British truck range from Fordson to Thames, and the ET's bonnet had a Thames badge with the Fordson name above it in smaller sized lettering. The ET was available in two standard lengths - 128-inch short wheelbase chassis, which allowed a 29/30-seat coach or the 157-inch long wheelbase for a 33/34-seater. Unusually, the bodies were of different styles - the shorter one having an almost straight waist rail, whilst the 33/34-seater had a waist and roof line which dipped from the door to the rear and looked very much like the back end of the half-cab body. Two engines were offered - the ET6 had the 3,622cc Ford V8 petrol (proven and smooth but thirsty) and the ET7 the Perkins P6 diesel (economical but noisy). So far as is known all but one of the coaches were ET6 models although several were retro-fitted with the Ford 4D 4.6-litre diesel engine, introduced in 1953.

However, one took on the combined might of General Motors (which owned Bedford) and Duple (turning out almost 1,000 coach bodies a year) at one's peril. That the Fordson did not achieve the success that it probably deserved was due to the aggressive pricing of the new Bedford/Duple Vega. At £2,190 it was the same as the price of a 29-seat Vista, which made the buy decision a very simple one for any operator - *"same money, four more seats"*. Moreover, Ford had no interest in building bus and coach chassis at the time, considering that the United Kingdom market was too small to warrant its attention. Several years later Ford of Britain did make a full-size coach chassis and there was an industry joke that it could produce all the UK's coach requirements in one afternoon shift at Dagenham.

The third design in the complete range was a neat little midibus. Drawings were made but so far as we have been able to determine none were built.

The fourth and principal design was for underfloor-engined chassis and Alec Hartwell was ready with something really modern, fashionable and up to date. He named it the Landmaster. Correctly he determined that coach bodies for these chassis would need to be metal-framed and he invested considerable effort and money to produce something of really high quality. It was a confident move for a relatively small coachbuilder - almost none of the smaller coachbuilders had steel-framed bodies but the large firms, such as Duple and Burlingham, were developing them and Duple's Vega body (for the new Bedford SB), Ambassador and Roadmaster (both for underfloor-engined chassis) were being designed with steel frames.

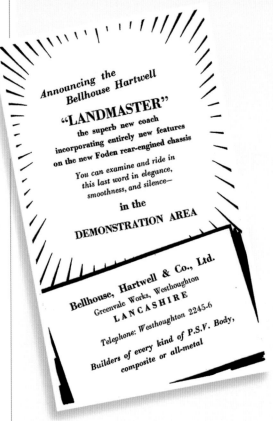

Announcing the Bellhouse Hartwell "LANDMASTER" the superb new coach incorporating entirely new features on the new Foden rear-engined chassis

You can examine and ride in this last word in elegance, smoothness, and silence—

in the

DEMONSTRATION AREA

Bellhouse, Hartwell & Co., Ltd.
Greenvale Works, Westhoughton
LANCASHIRE
Telephone: Westhoughton 2245-6
Builders of every kind of P.S.V. Body, composite or all-metal

Jesson (trading as Meredith & Jesson) of Cefn Mawr, Wrexham, bought Landmaster HCA 650 in September 1951. On an AEC Regal IV chassis, it was the last of the 1951 production.

On 21st August 1965 Roy Marshall took this picture of it operating its Cefn-Wrexham stage service.

The Landmaster proved very durable and most ran for a full 14 or 15-year lifespan; HCA 650 spent all its life with Meredith & Jesson, finally being withdrawn in 1969.

ROY MARSHALL

The Transatlantic - soon shortened to Atlantic - was innovative and ingenious. The aim was to achieve maximum seating capacity on a forward-engined chassis, with a virtually flat floor throughout the coach and all seats at the same level. It used the Foden PVFE6 chassis with its Foden two-stroke diesel engine - front-mounted and set low in the chassis, it was of much lower overall height than a normal four-stroke unit.

With some ingenuity - principally a noticeable bulge in the roof to give headroom above the engine, over which the floor had to be raised slightly - it could seat 39 on a 27ft 6in coach (which normally would carry 33).

Alec Hartwell was much influenced by American vehicle styling and there are signs of this in the porthole windows and single-pane windscreen. It is hard to describe the result as anything other than ugly.

The first was shown to the trade press in January 1950. Finished in Smith's livery, it was used as a demonstrator before going to Smith's in April, registered JP 8143. Smith's took two more, JP 8631/32, the chassis of the second had originally been ordered by Westbury Coaches of Westbury near Bristol. Smith's own order for a further chassis was changed to a Foden rear-engined chassis and became the prototype Landmaster, JP 8633.

Designing a good metal-framed coach body for underfloor-engined chassis needed not only skills but also considerable experience. Alec Hartwell head-hunted Massey Brothers' Chief Draughtsman, Edgar Evans, and his assistant Alan Lee. Evans had previously worked for Colin Bailey at Leyland. Colin Bailey was the country's foremost designer of metal-framed bus bodies. His first was in 1932 for Metropolitan-Cammell and it made that firm a major bus body builder. He was then headhunted by Leyland to redesign its initial, unsuccessful effort - the result was the hugely successful and attractive-looking Leyland double-deck body. Bailey moved to Duple early in 1948 to take that firm into metal-framing. At the same time, Edgar Evans joined Massey Brothers to do something similar for that firm's bus bodies. The Landmaster's frame used Evans' modification of the Leyland body frame section.

It was designed for quantity production rather than one-by-one custom build - something very different from the approach of most small or medium sized coachbuilders. Parts were made in batches and placed in the stores ready for assembly. After the 1950 prototype, 60 Landmasters were built - 19 in 1951, 17 in 1952, 12 in 1953 and 12 in 1954/55 - with parts for ten or so more in the stores when production ended. Chassis, including the prototype, were Leyland Royal Tiger (26) and Tiger Cub (3), AEC Regal IV (11) and Reliance (3), Daimler Freeline (8), Foden PVR (8) and Sentinel SLC (2).

Alec Hartwell had great plans for the Landmaster, hoping to sell it in quantity to the BET group and major independent coach operators such as Wallace Arnold. However, with the growing availability of private cars, the market for new coaches weakened considerably. Gaining orders, particularly from medium- and large-sized operators, became very tough with prices very keen.

Also, the big coachbuilding firms such as Duple, Burlingham and Plaxton had excellent links with the large operating groups and companies and did not give up their market share easily. For example, the well-known Scout Motor Services Ltd of Preston had been a Duple coach customer since 1937. It bought six Landmasters in 1951 along with eight bodies by Duple, all on Leyland Royal Tiger chassis. It is certain that a result was that Scout got some close attention from the Duple sales team with attractive offers to ensure future orders went to Duple - which they did.

In 1951 other well-established coachbuilders such as Windover and Whitson, the former having previously received substantial contracts from the BET group, were finding the market hard going and they, along with names such as Dutfield, Gurney Nutting, Longford, Santus, Trans United, Heaver and many others would soon give up coachbuilding, as would Bellhouse Hartwell. Equally importantly, the excitement of aerospace was beckoning Alec Hartwell.

However in 1949, whilst work was proceeding on the new designs, the Wigan coach operators wanted something different for the forward-engined Leyland PS1, PS2 and AEC Regal III chassis they had on order - and they wanted it quickly. The result was Beccols' Roadmaster and, somewhat later, Bellhouse Hartwell's Monarch.

THE LAST WORD IN LUXURY TRAVEL

THE FIRST OF TWO BODIES OF THIS TYPE. TO THE ORDER OF GREATREX COACHES LTD., STAFFORD

MOUNTED TO FODEN 2 STROKE DIESEL ENGINED CHASSIS

HEAVER LTD.
DURRINGTON. WILTS.
FROM 1897— Phone 256 —TO 1950

FODEN — DAIMLER
LEYLAND — DENNIS
GUY — ETC.

Heaver built just two Transatlantics under licence - both for Greatrex of Stafford in 1950.
PETER TULLOCH COLLECTION

The Atlantic

There were detail differences in the Atlantic bodies - the first four having a more upright front incorporating the grille that Foden supplied with the chassis, shown clearly in these pictures of EDB 14 and JP 8631 on this page, and LKA 718 and GBU 180 on the following pages.

ROY MARSHALL

Topping's Super Coaches of Liverpool took its brand new LKA 718 to the Rugby League Cup Final at Wembley in April 1950. It was one of the "upright" front Atlantics.

NA3T/A HUSTWITT

Eddie Holden bought two Atlantics, GBU 179 and 180, for his Shaw of Oldham fleet. The picture below shows GBU 180 for sale with dealer Stanley Hughes, Bradford, in April 1961, having passed to Gott of Bradford in 1958. This shows how the result was (apart from the bulge in the roof) not much higher than the adjacent forward-engined Daimler and rear-engined Foden.

J S COCKSHOTT ARCHIVE

In 1949 Bellhouse Hartwell was granted a patent for the Atlantic's design and then offered to license it to other coach builders. Heaver and Whitson both bought licences. Whitson did not proceed further and Heaver built only two - both for Greatrex of Stafford in 1950. Of the same general styling, Heaver's flat-front looked even uglier than the Bellhouse Hartwell.

PETER TULLOCH COLLECTION

31

The Fordson

This was a Ford-based version of the popular 29-seat Bedford/Duple Vista, then being phased out in favour of the Bedford SB-based 33-seater.

The chassis was the newly introduced Fordson Thames ET which was available in two standard lengths enabling a 29/30 or 33/34 seater coach.

Two engines were offered - the ET6 had Ford's 3,622cc V8 petrol unit (proven and smooth but thirsty) and the ET7 Perkins P6 diesel (economical but noisy). It seems all but one of the coaches were petrol when new.

These pictures are of the 30-seat prototype which was new in 1950. First used as a demonstrator it was sold to Slack, Blackpool and registered EFR 627 later that year.

PETER TULLOCH COLLECTION

By and large, Bellhouse Hartwell built standard products and did not do specials, but it could hardly decline a request from the Ford Motor Company for a coach for the Ford works band. Below the raised rear section was a large boot to carry the band's instruments.

Delivered in September 1950 RPU 509 was the second of the Fordsons to be built. Although offered as a standard product, it remained unique, although the raised-rear style had a smallish following in the industry.

PETER TULLOCH COLLECTION

The prototype had an unusual fully-glazed rear dome; spectacular in its way but not something which enhanced the view of many passengers. Most of the later examples had conventional domes.

PETER TULLOCH COLLECTION

In 1950 a solitary Fordson-style body was built on a wartime Bedford OWB chassis and ran for some nine years for Dodds of Troon. It seems likely it was assembled from parts in the stores, as it had a glazed rear dome like the prototype Fordson.

R P DOIG

The 33/34-seat body differed from the 29/30-seater. It had a dipping waist rail and looked much the same as the rear part of the half-cab design.

Reeve of Rubery in Worcestershire bought two - LOE 701/2 but specified only 30 seats. LOE 701 later passed to Seatax of Paignton.

The 4D badge on the grille of LOE 701 in the picture above indicates that its original V8 petrol engine had been replaced with Ford's 4D 3.6-litre diesel, introduced in 1953. A careful look at the picture shows the two pairs of a different type of seat which Seatax added, bringing the seating up to 34.

The large (33/34 seat) and small (29/30 seat) version of the Fordson differed in styling, although both had the slender window pillars enabled by the steel vertical body framing. The prototype small version, EFR 627, is seen above in 1964 after it had passed to Wilson of Carnwath in 1959.

IAIN MACGREGOR

Large LMU 605 was new to Friern Mental Hospital, London, and later, as here, passed into preservation for a time.

CHRIS HOWARD

Parts for 15 Fordsons were made but, with the introduction of the Big Bedford SB, these coaches were not easy to sell. Several went to provide useful service as transport for homes and settlements for the disabled and handicapped.

The Devon Mental Hospital Management Committee bought OHW 407 in 1952. Much later, the coach had a spectacular end when owned by Bickers of Codenham as part of his 'fleet' used in TV stunts - it was overturned and wrecked in an episode of the ITV series Heartbeat.

MICHAEL DRYHURST

TEV 910 went to the Brentwood Mental Hospital in Essex in August 1951. It, too, has had its petrol engine replaced by a Ford 4D diesel.

GEOFF MILLS

And this was the reason they were hard to sell - the 33-seat Bedford SB/Duple Vega was aggressively priced at £2197, exactly the same as a 29-seat Bedford OB/Duple Vista. That price made buying an easy decision for small and medium sized operators, and it killed the market for Bellhouse Hartwell's Fordson - one took on the combination of General Motors and Duple at one's peril.

On the right is Hanson of Huddersfield's Vega FVH 411 which was new in 1952 but still in good order when this picture was taken in 1962.

J S COCKSHOTT ARCHIVE

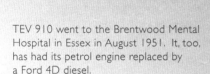

BELLHOUSE . HARTWELL & CO LTD

EMERGENCY DOOR

26 SEAT BODY ON SEDDON
CHASSIS

SCALE ⅛ in 1 FOOT
4 DEC 1950

The third part of Alec Hartwell's complete range
would have been this neat 26-seat midibus -
this drawing shows it on a Seddon Mk7P chassis.
So far as is known, none were built.

The drawing seems to show wooden-slatted seats,
presumably for industrial or site work.

The Landmaster

When 30ft underfloor-engined chassis were announced, Alec Hartwell determined that coach bodies for these would need to be metal-framed and he invested in a design of high quality. The result was the Landmaster.

It was a confident move for a relatively small coachbuilder - almost none of the smaller coachbuilders had steel-framed bodies and the large firms, such as Duple and Burlingham, were only just developing them - Duple's Vega body (for the new Bedford SB), Ambassador and Roadmaster (both for underfloor-engined chassis) were to have steel frames.

This needed new skills and direct experience and he recruited Massey Brothers' Chief Draughtsman Edgar Evans, who had previously worked for Colin Bailey at Leyland. Bailey was responsible for Metropolitan-Cammell's very successful steel-framed bus body, moving on to Leyland in 1935 - Leyland's first attempt had proved less than good and it headhunted Bailey to redesign it. In 1948 he moved to Duple to take that firm into metal-framing, and Evans went to Massey to do something similar for that firm's bus bodies.

The result was smart, assertive and confident at a time when the styling of underfloor-engined coaches was generally somewhat uncertain.

The first, once again for Smith's of Wigan, was a late entry in the demonstration park at the 1950 Commercial Motor Show. Built on a rear-engined Foden PVRF6 chassis and subsequently registered JP 8633 following on from the last two Atlantics, JP 8631/32, it was changed by Smith's from an order for a third Atlantic.

BELLHOUSE HARTWELL ARCHIVE
via RAY STENNING

The styling of underfloor-engined coaches proved difficult for designers. Early attempts, such as Duple's, tried to retain some semblance of a driver's cab area, dividing the side window line with a thickened pillar.

The first really successful design, treating the body as a single harmonious entity, was Burlingham's Seagull. It sold very well and increased Burlingham's share of the market.

This is Ribble 951, a Leyland Tiger Cub, one of 15 new in 1954. Bellhouse Hartwell copied the Seagull's side mouldings on the Landmaster Mark IV.

J S COCKSHOTT ARCHIVE

Orders for the Landmaster followed quickly. The production version, named the Landmaster Mark II, had a sliding passenger door and slightly different detailing from the prototype, which was named the Mark I and continued only on Foden rear-engined chassis. There were options on the arrangement of the polished aluminium trim.

Delivery began in March 1951 with Mark I MTJ 29, a Foden PVRF6 for Taylor of Leigh, as shown on the right.

NA3T/A HUSTWITT

The first on an AEC Regal IV chassis was EWH 168 for Knowles of Bolton, shown below.

PETER GREAVES

New in June, KWT 978, shown above, was a Leyland Royal Tiger for the well-known Yorkshire operator Ripponden & District Motors Ltd. 20 Landmasters had been delivered by the end of the season.

ROY MARSHALL

Proud of their product, in the picture at the top right the works team posed with EWH 168.

ALLAN LEE

All Bellhouse Hartwell's interiors had similar styling - the picture to the right shows the interior of JP 8633.

BELLHOUSE HARTWELL ARCHIVE

Scout Motor Services of Preston had six Lansmasters on Leyland Royal Tiger chassis (DRN 363, 926-930). One of them is shown below.

BELLHOUSE HARTWELL ARCHIVE

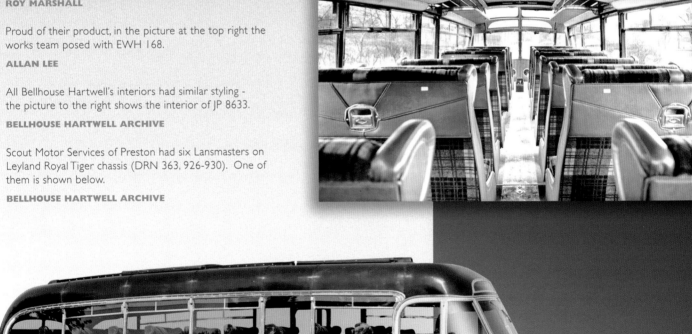

The majority of Landmasters were on Leyland Royal Tiger chassis and here are two in later life. NTC 445 on the right was new to Oliver Hart of Coppull, near Wigan, and passed to A & C McLennan of Spittalfield, Perth, when Hart closed down his bus and coach operations.

This picture shows it in North William Street, Perth, on 23rd June 1963 with McLennan. It joined the McLennan fleet in 1958 and ran with them until 1970. The two pictures show the differing styles of trim used on the front of the early Landmaster bodies.

IAIN MACGREGOR

GBU 729 was new to Renton, Hollinwood, Oldham, and went thence to Elsworth of Blackpool, in whose red and grey livery it is seen below in 1964.

BRIAN LEWIS via DON AKRIGG

Although for many years they had been the norm in the United States and for many service bus bodies in the United Kingdom, steel-framed coach bodies were relatively new to the British market and there was some nervousness about their adoption - the transport industry had a conservative outlook. They were also more costly than coach bodies with composite (steel/timber) framing.

Duple's Vega, Ambassador and Roadmaster were steel-framed. The first two were styled by Duple's long-serving designer but the Roadmaster was by Bailey. It usurped the name used by Beccols, but Duple was mighty and there was nothing that tiny Beccols could do, not having registered it.

Here are the two Bailey designs - Leyland's coach body and Duple's Roadmaster. Aft of the front axle the designs had a family resemblance.

The Leyland body sold the most, but only as a result of a large bulk order from the BET group, mainly for Ribble. The Roadmaster was not Duple's most attractive design and did not sell well.

The Leyland body, like the Landmaster, could suffer from water leaks around the windscreen and some of the Ribble/Standerwick fleet had the modification (a rubber flap), as shown in the picture at the top of Standerwick 153.

Standerwick and Scout both had a small number of Duple Roadmasters. Scout had three plus 11 Ambassadors, in addition to its six Landmasters. Scout Roadmaster DRN 356 later passed to the immaculate fleet of R J Prescott & Sons' Bamber Bridge Motor Services, near Preston, as seen in the middle picture.

Scout's first five Ambassadors were DRN 358-62. The last of them, in the bottom picture, was still in fine condition in 1961, by which time it and DRN 358 and 360 had passed to Tom Jackson of Chorley.

Interestingly, union pressure and operator resistance caused Duple to revert to composite frames for its later Ambassadors and Vegas.

J S COCKSHOTT ARCHIVE

Two Landmaster-style bodies were built
on forward-engined chassis and differed according to the
version of the Landmaster on which each was modelled - changes in
Landmaster styling are covered in the illustrations of chapter eight.

JTE 792 was a Leyland PS1 belonging to Hodgson of Morecambe.
New in 1948 its Santus body was not one of that firm's best efforts,
so it received the Landmaster body shown at the top.

ROY MARSHALL

With the Landmaster, Alec Hartwell had a full range of coach bodies,
which he described in the letter on the right that he wrote to the Bus
and Coach correspondent, hoping for some publicity in that trade magazine.

Like the interior, the design of the rear of the Landmaster followed the
general Bellhouse Hartwell house style. Below is the rear of Hebble 33.
When new it had been numbered 71.

TREVOR HARTLEY

John F. Speed Esq.,
5, Orchard Lane,
Wimbledon,
London, S.W.20.

14th November, 1951.

Dear Mr. Speed,

Herewith photographs of one of the 18 'Landmaster' Mark III bodies
which we are building for Messrs. Blue Cars (Continental) Ltd. of 224,
Shaftesbury Avenue, London, W.C.2, on Leyland Royal Tiger 30' x 8'
chassis.

This body has a riveted steel structure of great strength and, under
separate cover, we have sent two drawings which show the arrangement of
pillars and crossbearers.

Some special features of this vehicle are:-

1. Forced draught ventilation. Air is taken through water-proof
vents in the front canopy (photographs 12849 & 50) and driven
by two double centrifugal fans along ducts at each side of the
coach. Each seat has an adjustable aircraft type louvre by
means of which the passengers can regulate the direction and
quantity of incoming air. When the coach is in motion, the
system works without the fans.

2. The front o/s door combines the duties of emergency, driver's
and passengers' door. This is particularly useful when the
vehicle stops on the right-hand side of the road. Photograph
12852 illustrates the step arrangement.

3. 32 large armchair seats are fitted with extra deep Dunlopillo
cushions, squabs and headrests and have folding central arm-
rests. A single swivelling seat is provided for the courier.

-2-

4. Hassock type footrests are provided and can be positioned
for each passengers maximum comfort.

5. Curtains are fitted to all side and roof windows.

6. As shown on the pillar arrangement drawing, the side and
rear windows are fitted from the outside of the vehicle
and may be removed without a major disturbance of the
trimming.

7. Heel discs with air flow louvres are fitted.

I believe I have already given you photographs of our 'Landmaster'
Mark II bodies which are identical with the above but have a slightly
different wing design. Like the Mark III they may be fitted with up
to 41 seats. Photograph No.12656 herewith illustrates this model on
an A.E.C. Mark IV chassis with 41 seats, operated by Messrs. Meredith
& Jesson of Cefn Mawr near Wrexham. This body is suitable for all
under-floor or rear-engined chassis.

Our body for all forward engine chassis is the 'Monarch' which
gives to this type of chassis something of the appearance of an under-
floor or rear-engined coach. It can be fitted with up to 39 luxury
seats. I believe you already have photographs 11308, 11309 & 11310A
illustrating this type of body on a Tilling Stevens chassis, fitted with
33 seats and supplied to Messrs. Newquay Motor Co. Ltd., Newquay, Cornwall.

We also build coach bodies for Fordson chassis which may be fitted
with either petrol or 6 cylinder diesel engines. There are three models:-

1. The standard 29/30 seater. (Photograph No.11679, already in your
possession, of a coach supplied to Messrs. Ganson Bros. Ltd.
Lerwick, Shetland.)

2. A similar coach with a longer wheelbase, seating 33/34
passengers.

3. A 1½ deck, 33/34 seat coach with very large luggage space.
(Photographs 11311 & 11312 already in your possession show
a coach of this type built for the use of the Ford Motor Co.
Ltd., Dagenham.)

If you are short of any of the above photographs or if there is any
further information you require, please do not hesitate to let us know.

Faithfully yours,
BELLHOUSE, HARTWELL & CO. LTD.

Director.

Smith's of Wigan Leyland PS1 JP 7221 started life in 1948 with a Pearson body. This did not prove durable and in 1952 it was sent to Greenvale for a new Bellhouse Hartwell body. Here it is on the right in later life, in August 1957, with Ledgard of Leeds. Although nicely polished, the dark blue and black livery makes the picture dark.

Ledgard also acquired some of Smith's Beccols-bodied AEC Regals - in the top picture is JP 8146 in April 1957.

J S COCKSHOTT ARCHIVE

Pots, pans & pedal cars

Alongside coach production, the metal-forming business thrived. Belso Ware tea sets, pans, stepladders and a range of children's pedal cars were sold through Bellhouse Higson, using the Bellhouse home address for marketing.

Pans and similar items were supplied in very large quantities to major retail stores such as Woolworth's - at the time a major High Street name. To the left is some of the pubplicity for these. Even the polished wheel trims of the coaches were a Greenvale product.

BELLHOUSE HARTWELL ARCHIVE

Lightweight aluminium stepladders were another product line. In the background of the picture at the bottom left several hundred Belso Ware pans are stacked, packed and ready for delivery.

BELLHOUSE HARTWELL ARCHIVE

Another product line was a range of pedal cars for children. In the picture below a young Kim Kynaston, Fred Bellhouse's grandson, is at the wheel of his *De-Luxe Streamline* in 1956. One of Alec's daughters - Penny and Carol - modelled for the pictures of the jeep.

Both (having long grown out of pedal cars) kindly contributed memories and archives for this book.

BELLHOUSE FAMILY ARCHIVE, KIM KYNASTON

Commercials

To offset the seasonal demand for coaches, Greenvale built a fair number of commercial bodies - like Beccols, many were for Bromilow and Edwards. Here are four examples of non-Bromilow and Edwards work.

On the left in the colour pictures are two fire tenders for the Bolton fire brigade built in 1951/52, below is a Bedford van for Procter and Gamble's washing and cleaning products division and, finally in the small picture is PTC 61, the splendid coach-styled Bellhouse Hartwell works van - it was an Austin.

There was also the increasingly important aircraft work, covered in a later chapter; it became the company's principal business from 1952.

The firm's wide diversification was in contrast to Beccols, resulting from the hard times experienced in the cotton trade and the risks of having to rely on a single, narrow market.

BELLHOUSE HARTWELL ARCHIVE

chapter 5
Something distinctive

In 1949/1950, with the initial demand for coaches satisfied, there was a growing need for something more attractive than the half-cab coach. Full-width front coaches became the fashion and most of the major coachbuilders - Burlingham, Plaxton and Duple had examples at the 1948 Commercial Motor Show, although most were simply a full-width cab added to an existing half-cab design.

At the time, one of the largest private coach operators in the North West was James Smith & Co (Wigan) Ltd, owned by less well-known Webster Brothers (Wigan) Ltd. A key part of Smith's operations was continental tours - something that many large operators offered in the days before the jet engine and packaged air holidays - and Smith's had very firm requirements for the vehicles used on these. Good forward vision was one and this was something that the half-cab or even a full-front design with a full-height bulkhead behind the driver did not offer. Smith's asked its two local coachbuilders to produce something - the result was Beccols' Roadmaster and, slightly later, Bellhouse Hartwell's Monarch.

Beccols first Roadmaster coaches were built in the middle of 1949 on lightweight Austin chassis which had been converted from normal-control to forward-control. The full-front bodies featured windows in the front dome, D-shaped 'cab' windows and no full-height bulkhead behind the driver. The appearance was striking and very much in keeping with George Nichol's style. They had Bolton registration numbers but went to Butterworth (Pathfinder) of Blackpool - and quickly featured in Beccols' advertisement for the new design.

Underfloor-engined chassis might be on the horizon, as might Bellhouse Hartwell's Atlantic, but in the short term Smith's needed up-to-date fashionable bodies to maintain its place in the market and needed something like this for the heavyweight Leyland PS1, PS2, AEC Regal III and Crossley SD42 chassis which it had on order. It placed orders for ten bodies from Beccols (eight AEC Regals and two Leyland PS2s) and six from Bellhouse Hartwell (three AEC Regal, one Crossley SD42, one Leyland PS1, one Leyland PS2).

Eliminating the full-height bulkhead partition behind the driver needed careful design. Coach bodies on a full-sized chassis relied on this bulkhead for strength and rigidity. Beccols cantilevered the cab area off the main body and Bellhouse Hartwell did something similar. On both bodies the

Tour	Days	Tours Leaving GOOD FRIDAY and EVERY SATURDAY	£ s. d
1	7 Days	Brighton-Torquay (Sunny South Coast) Weymouth	14 14 0
2	7 "	Bournemouth, Festival of Britain and Weymouth	14 14 0
3	7 "	Ilfracombe (North Devon, Clovelly, Lynton, Lynmouth)	14 14 0
4	7 "	London (Windsor, Brighton and Festival of Britain)	14 7 6
5	7 "	Edinburgh (The Trossachs and Melrose)	14 14 0
6	9 "	Newquay (Land's End, St. Ives, Falmouth)	19 10 0
7	9 "	Scottish Highlands (Edinburgh, Pitlochry, Oban)	19 10 0
8	9 "	John O'Groats (Royal Route, Inverness-Edinburgh)	19 10 0
9	9 "	Isle of Wight, Folkestone, Festival of Britain	19 10 0

SMITH'S TOURS

HOLIDAYS IN GREAT BRITAIN AND ABROAD

● Luxury Travel   ● First Class Coaches   ● Fares Fully Inclusive

ANNOUNCING OUR 1951 PROGRAMME

Tours Leaving GOOD FRIDAY and EVERY MONDAY

Tour	Days		£ s. d
10	7 Days	West and East Coast (Caernarvon, Aberystwyth, Great Yarmouth)	16 0 0
11	7 "	Land's End (Newquay, Ilfracombe, Llandrindod Wells)	16 0 0
12	7 "	Edinburgh, Pitlochry, Ayreshire Coast (Steamer trip to Kyles of Bute)	16 10 0
13	7 "	John O'Groats (Royal Route, Inverness-Edinburgh)	16 0 0
14	7 "	Norfolk Broads, Festival of Britain, Wales	16 0 0
15	5 "	London (Windsor and Festival of Britain)	10 0 0
16	5 "	Scottish Lochs (2 nights in Callander, and 2 nights in Edinburgh)	10 10 0
17	5 "	Ilfracombe (North Devon, Clovelly)	10 10 0
18	5 "	Somerset (Isle of Wight, Cheddar Gorge)	10 10 0
19	5 "	Bude (North Devon, Clovelly, Lynton)	10 10 0
20	5 "	Isle of Anglesey, Bangor, Caernarvon, Llandrindod Wells, Wye Valley	10 10 0

Tour			£ s. d
A	14 Days	Switzerland (staying 6 nights at the Palace Hotel, Lucerne), visiting Paris, Interlaken, Trummelbach Falls, Fluelen, Basle, Vittel, Dijon	55 0 0
B	14 "	Switzerland (staying 7 nights at the Palace Hotel, Montreux), visiting Paris, Sens, Geneva, Chateau D'Oex, Gruyere, Dijon	55 0 0
C	16 "	Belgium, Holland, Germany and Denmark, visiting Dusseldorf, Hamburg, Odense, Copenhagen, Flesburg, Groningen, Amsterdam, Breda	65 0 0
D	16 "	Spain, visiting Rouen, Poitiers, Biarritz, San Sebastian, Burgos, Madrid, Valencia, Barcelona, Carcassone, Angouleme, Paris	65 0 0
E	16 "	Road to Rome, visiting Rheims, Montreux, Stresa, Florence, Rome, Pisa, Nice, Grenoble, Vichy, Paris	65 0 0
F	14 "	Biarritz (staying 7 nights at the Miramar Hotel, Biarritz), visiting Paris, Chartres, Tours, Rouen, Bordeaux, Pau. Excursions into Spain to San Sebastian and Pamplona	55 0 0
G	14 "	French Riviera (staying 6 nights at the Ruhl Hotel, Nice), visiting Cannes, Monte Carlo, Lyon, Rheims, Paris, San Remo, Grenoble, Avallon, Auxerre	55 0 0
P	9 "	Paris (staying 5 nights at the Lutetia Hotel, Paris), visiting Versailles, and the beautiful forest and Chateau of Fontainebleau. Arrangements are made by our Courier for visits to the Folies Bergere, Bal Tabrin and the Lido. Tour of the city night life	32 0 0

ADVANCE BOOKINGS HAVE NOW COMMENCED

James Smith & Co. (Wigan), Ltd., 70, Market Street, Wigan, Lancashire.   Telephone : Wigan 44246

Beccols first Roadmaster bodies were on two Austin K4 chassis, converted to forward-control. DBN 919/20 were delivered to Butterworth (Pathfinder) of Blackpool in June of 1949.

The indicator boxes fitted below a higher-set windscreen were not repeated on subsequent bodies.

Beccols lost no time in publicising its new design. The "eternal triangle" was maybe a little corny and the text somewhat over the top but with its reference to a wide range of designs this 1949 advertisement for the Roadmaster nicely captured what Beccols was about.

NICHOLS ARCHIVE

radiator cowl, normally exposed,
was concealed behind a styled front panel.
The Roadmaster's front dome had two large windows, either side of a small peak and, on most bodies, a circular illuminated medallion with the operator's logo or initials. There was the usual sliding roof but with two opening sections. A pair of windows in the rear dome seems to have been an option. Apart from the first Blue Cars Royal Tiger, all Beccols' 1950-season production was Roadmasters.

Bellhouse Hartwell's design had a fully-glazed cab but the corners were squared off and the result was, perhaps, rather less refined than that of Beccols. The design was then improved with gently rounded D-shaped wrap-around corner windows for the cab which were of a more subtle shape than those of Beccols - the prototype was built in 1950. Both firms' bodies then had similar frontal treatment using polished aluminium strips and were so similar that at first glance it was confusing as to whose was which. Rearwards from the cab the styling of both was much the same as the half-cab.

In the late 1940s and early 1950s there was an upsurge in continental touring using coaches with fewer seats, better visibility and high quality trim. Smith's of Wigan were an important operator and its requirements strongly influenced Beccols and, to a lesser degree, Bellhouse Hartwell. This advertisement for the 1951 season featured Beccols-bodied Leyland PS2 JP 8051 - one of two, JP 8050/51, delivered in 1949 along with six similarly bodied AEC Regal IIIs, JP 8145-50 in 1950.

PETER TULLOCH COLLECTION

Beccols' first 'full-size, no-bulkhead' Roadmaster was JP 7866, an AEC Regal III delivered to Smith's of Wigan in September 1949. Equipped with just 15 luxurious seats upholstered in soft leather, it went at once to a trade show in Nice, where it attracted great attention.

Beccols produced the marketing postcard shown below - complete with a French road repair going on.

The rear of the coach was signwritten with Smith's continental destinations - Switzerland, Germany, France, Belgium, Italy and Spain, shown at the bottom of the opposite page.

JP 8147 had 25 individual reclining seats, again upholstered in soft leather but this was purely for the rally and, like JP 7866, the coach was soon altered to its licensed 31 seating.

To make it easy and safe for passengers boarding and alighting when across the channel, the offside emergency door was fitted with steps which folded out from the body when the door was opened - Beccols registered the design. You can see the steps in the picture in the Commercial Motor advert on the opposite page.

NICHOLS ARCHIVE

The first full-sized coaches went to Smith's in September 1949 - Beccols bodied JP 7866 and Bellhouse Hartwell built JP 7884, both were AEC Regals. The design became the standard for forward-engined chassis for both coachbuilders. Beccols named its version the "Roadmaster" from the start but it was a year later that Bellhouse Hartwell followed suit naming its 1950 models with the D-shaped wrap-around corner windows the "Monarch". Beccols did not register the Roadmaster name and Duple would very shortly use it for one version of its metal-framed underfloor-engined coach body. Beccols may have complained but had more pressing problems described in the following chapters. Even so, big companies usually win.

Smith's JP 7866 was luxuriously fitted-out for continental touring with fifteen individual reclining seats upholstered in soft leather and was taken to Nice, France, to show to the tours market in September of 1949. Next year, Smith's brand new similar JP 8147, this time seating 25, was entered in the International Coach Rally at Montreux, Switzerland, in May 1950. It won second prize overall for its coachwork - the winner was a Windover-bodied Regal of Sheffield United Tours - another major player in continental touring. Win that SUT coach might - SUT was a previous winner at such events and "knew the ropes" - but its full-front body really was of a previous generation. Although very well fitted out, it was the standard Windover half-cab design, modified with a full-width cab but with the radiator cowl exposed and a full-height bulkhead behind the driver.

Beccols' new design attracted orders. A notable one was from Barton Transport, Chilwell, Nottingham, for four bodies on widely different chassis which were modified either by Barton or Beccols to Barton's instruction. Their bodies had a revised frontal design with a more pronounced dip to the wrap-around 'cab' windows, eliminating the D-shape. Both style variations were delivered to subsequent customers. The Beccols style was copied on some later bodies built in-house by Barton and one built for Barton by Massey.

Beccols built 48 Roadmaster-style bodies (8 in 1949, 31 in 1950, 8 in 1951 and 1 in 1952) whereas the Monarch and its full-front no-bulkhead predecessor seems to have been something of a diversion for Bellhouse Hartwell, which built a combined total of only 31 of its two designs (3 in 1949, 12 in 1950, 10 in 1951 and 6 in 1952), preferring to hold to its standard product line whilst designing the Atlantic, Landmaster and Fordson.

The Roadmaster and Monarch would quickly be history. After the 1950 Commercial Motor Show hardly anyone placed orders for heavyweight forward-engined coaches - the future was underfloor-engined chassis.

33 SEATER LUXURY COACH
By BECCOLS LTD. Chequerbent, Bolton, Lancashire

Beccols
Roadmaster

Aiming to capitalise on the impact it made at Nice, in November Beccols placed a full page advertisement in the Commercial Motor. The reference to Series C was pure marketing.

PETER GREAVES COLLECTION

In May 1950 JP 8147, one of six AEC Regals for Smith's (JP 8145-50), was entered in the International Coach Rally at Montreux in Switzerland where it won second prize.

The winner was a Sheffield United Regal with a Windover body - nicely fitted out but still basically a half-cab design modified with a full front through which the radiator shell was exposed - contrasting with the Roadmaster with its styled front, no bulkhead between driver and passengers, and windows in the front dome. Sheffield United, however, had a track record of winning at this rally.

NICHOLS ARCHIVE

Two Beccols-bodied coaches were ordered by Isle of Man operators. MMN 85, shown on the left, was an Albion Victor for Collister of Douglas. The other, illustrated in chapter 12, was a normal-control Leyland Comet for Kneen, also of Douglas.

Beccols bodied two of the relatively rare Morris Commercial chassis. Diesel-engined OP GFY 716, on the opposite page at the bottom, was lettered for Howard of Blackpool but went to the associated Whiteside, also of Blackpool. The other was KUF 15, a petrol-engined PP for Hart (Alpha) of Brighton, which, shown on the right, was photographed posed on the town's Madeira Drive.

The Nice trip attracted orders. Shortly after Smith's JP 8145-50, Beccols built two 25-seat Roadmasters for Bee-Line of West Hartlepool, again for continental work, as shown below. EF 9344/9369 were on AEC Regal chassis and had 2 +1 seating. They, too, were soon altered to the more usual seating arrangement - it was hard to make money with only 25 passengers.

Bee-Line Continental Tours.

52

53

Beccols won an order from the large (and very independent) firm of Barton Transport of Chilwell near Nottingham. Barton had a reputation for the unusual and its order for four coaches was completely in accord with this. Unlike Bellhouse Hartwell (and Barton's usual coachbuilder, Duple), Beccols was always willing to do specials.

Their front ends had no D-shape windows and a more pronounced dip of the wrap-around front windscreen.

First was LAL 849 - a normal-control Leyland Comet chassis that was rebuilt to forward-control before it was fitted with a 32-seat Roadmaster body with a sliding roof and high specification coach seating for long-distance touring. On the right is the coach when new.

NICHOLS ARCHIVE

It ended its days on bus service duties, as in the lower picture taken in Nottingham.

J S COCKSHOTT ARCHIVE

LNN 802 and LRR 691 were Barton BTS1 models. Barton's BTS1 was a 30ft-long chassis rebuilt from pairs of second-hand pre-war Leyland Titan chassis. They had 43-seat bodies with lower specification seats for express service work, like LNN 802 at Nottingham bound for Skegness.

NICHOLS ARCHIVE

Below is LRR 691 in Barton's garage yard in Chilwell.

ROY MARSHALL

The revised front end design was adopted for subsequent Roadmasters. Above is GDM 682, a Tilling Stevens K6LA7 delivered in January 1951 to Bellis of Buckley in Flint. It was in sparkling condition when photographed in London later that year on an excursion to the Festival of Britain.

NA3T/A HUSTWITT

Barton's third variant was LNN 886, shown on the right and below - a 27ft 6in Leyland Tiger PS2 chassis which Barton had lengthened to 30ft. Although it had glass panels down the full length of its roof and on into the rear dome, it had 43 express service seats.

NICHOLS ARCHIVE

Beccols bodied two AEC Regals for the Florence/Kia-Ora group of Morecambe. Although lettered for continental work, they seated 35. Licensed in August 1951, NTC 610/11 were two of the last Beccols bodies in work when the firm laid off most of its staff due to financial problems arising from the Blue Cars order. NTC 611 is shown on the left.

ROY MARSHALL

DDB 525, in the lower picture on the left, belonged to Cooper of Bredbury, on the outskirts of Stockport. It started life as a coach in January 1949 as one of the Beccols-bodied normal-control Commer Q4 wartime lorry chassis. At the end of the 1950 season Cooper rebuilt the chassis to forward-control and Beccols then fitted a Roadmaster front end to the existing body. .

ROY MARSHALL

Atkinson (General) of Chester-le-Street had two Beccols bodies on Crossley chassis. One was a half-cab and the other this Roadmaster below. It was new in 1950 and was still with General when this picture was taken in June 1958

J S COCKSHOTT ARCHIVE

57

There are very few colour pictures of Beccols-bodied coaches. Albion Victor MMN 85, shown above, was new to Collister of Douglas in 1950 and remained with Collister until May 1964 when the fleet was absorbed by Tours (IOM) Ltd.

Still in Collister's livery, it was sold to Lamb of Douglas who ran it until March 1967

GEOFF LUMB

AEC Regal JP 8148 was one of six bought by Smith's of Wigan for continental touring in 1950. Smith's ran it for five years and it then passed it to Bere Regis & District, Dorset, for whom it ran until it went for scrap in 1964. Here it is on the right in Bere Regis colours.

ARNOLD RICHARDSON

Bellhouse Hartwell Monarch

In September and October 1949 Bellhouse Hartwell delivered its first 'no-bulkhead' bodies - JP 7884 and 7962 for Smith's on AEC Regal III chassis. Although the body had the windows in the dome with the peak between them, the front end looked awkward, mainly because it used flat glass. JP 7962 is above. A more refined design using curved corner windows was introduced in 1950 and named Monarch.

ROY MARSHALL

Smith's, Beccols and Bellhouse Hartwell were ahead of the rest of the pack. Early in 1950 market-leader Duple produced a home market full-front no-bulkhead coach. For the Leeds-based Wallace Arnold fleet it was on a Leyland Tiger PS2 chassis and seated 21. Its first task was a promotional tour of the USA, as part of which it was exhibited at the April 1950 British Motor Show in New York - but its styling seemed to lack Duple's usual elegance. On return it was registered NUG 1. Then in 1953 Wallace Arnold removed the body and fitted it to 1947 Leyland Tiger PS1/1 chassis KUG 667, in which form it is shown in this picture on the left.

J S COCKSHOTT ARCHIVE

The styling was adapted to suit the Foden front grille of KYF 894, as you can see above, a PVSC6 for Ansell of London.

NA3T/A HUSTWITT

Another pre-Monarch was FDR 54, shown on the right - a Tilling Stevens K6LA7 chassis for Embankment of Plymouth delivered in 1950.

Embankment had two 1948 Maudslay Marathons rebodied with Monarchs in 1952, which replaced their original Whitson bodies.

R H G SIMPSON

The Bellhouse Hartwell Monarch had nicely styled cab windows and looked similar to the Beccols Roadmaster at first glance, as you can see when comparing these two pictures.

The top picture shows Beccols Roadmaster JP 8145, which had been sold in 1956 by Smith's to Berresford of Cheddleton in Staffordshire.

J S COCKSHOTT ARCHIVE

The first Monarch was NAF 509 shown below, a Tilling Stevens K6MA7 for the Newquay Motor Company in Cornwall, which chose not to have the windows in the front dome.

BELLHOUSE HARTWELL ARCHIVE

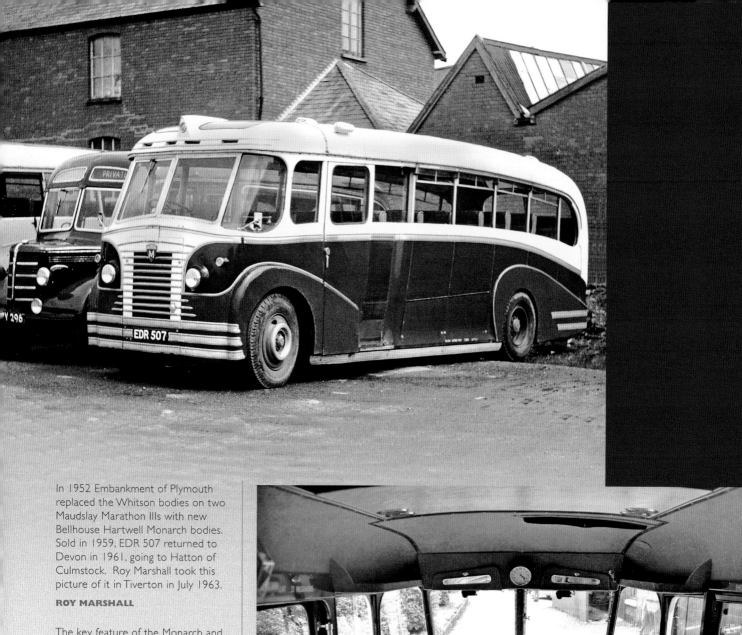

In 1952 Embankment of Plymouth replaced the Whitson bodies on two Maudslay Marathon IIIs with new Bellhouse Hartwell Monarch bodies. Sold in 1959, EDR 507 returned to Devon in 1961, going to Hatton of Culmstock. Roy Marshall took this picture of it in Tiverton in July 1963.

ROY MARSHALL

The key feature of the Monarch and Roadmaster was the elimination of the bulkhead partition between the driver and the passengers. It gave greatly increased visibility, requiring not only some ingenuity in the design of the framing but also the insulation of engine noise from the saloon and sealing against the possible intrusion of oil or fuel smells.

Just look at the beautifully detailed, high quality finish of NAF 509 - it maybe illustrates the difference from Beccols' 'good honest job' approach.

BELLHOUSE HARTWELL ARCHIVE

The final order for Monarch bodies was an important one, for it came from one of the major players in the coach industry, Wallace Arnold of Leeds. Its AEC Regal IIIs MUB 437/38 were new in 1949 with Burlingham C33F bodies. In 1952 these were removed for use elsewhere and the two chassis sent to Greenvale for fitting with 8ft-wide Monarch bodies. Restrictions on the use of 8ft-wide vehicles had meant that coaches were usually built to 7ft 6in width; they were eased with the authorising of 30ft × 8ft single-deckers in 1950.

The pair are shown on the right in September 1958, by which time MUB 437 had received some modification to the Bellhouse Hartwell (allegedly) "silent, rain proof" ventilation slots in the front dome.

J S COCKSHOTT ARCHIVE

Owned by Renton of Hollinwood, near Oldham, Monarch GBU 647 was one of the last Leyland PS1/1s built.

An identifying feature of the Monarch was the two strips of polished trim on the rear wing valence on later Bellhouse Hartwell bodies - Beccols had three.

MICHAEL TAYLOR

chapter 6
Blue Cars

If Smith's offered luxury touring then the service offered by Blue Cars (Continental) Ltd of 224 Shaftesbury Avenue, London was probably the ultimate. The firm was owned by Thomas Edwin (Ted) Langton with his younger brother Robert as a minority shareholder.

Born in 1904 in Southport and married to an Ormskirk girl, Ted Langton was always looking for something new and modern, similar to Alec Hartwell, and became a noted pioneer in the travel industry, developing novel approaches to holidays and building up substantial companies with a good reputation. When a company grew too large to control personally or when someone made a good offer, he would sell it and move on to a new venture. Dedicated and highly focussed, he was generous to those who supported him but could be volatile and intolerant of those who let him down.

His first venture was prompted by a conversation in a Liverpool pub with a coach owner who was complaining bitterly of the dearth of business. *"How much do you want if I hire a coach for the whole summer,"* he asked. Receiving an encouraging reply, he set off to the West Country to find hotels that were in similar need of customers. Having secured a similar deal he combined the two and called the company Happiway(s). The original week's inclusive holiday in 1931 cost just £5 - which made it very affordable. Although packaged tours had been around for some time, Ted Langton had invented the "one week in one place" packaged holiday.

As early as 1927 he had identified Spain as an important future holiday target and for some years ran the London-based Spanish Travel Bureau. With W R Bairstow he set up the Iberian Tourist Development Co Ltd ("Iberocars") in Liverpool in 1932, selling Happiway in 1933 and moving into continental packaged holidays. A Belgian company Les Cars Bleu was started that year and because of restrictions on using British coaches on the continent, coaches were hired from continental operators with travel from London to the continent by train and ferry. From 1936 the tours were marketed under the name Blue Cars, and Blue Cars (Continental) Ltd was registered in November 1937. Sold through agencies and widely advertised, they appeared to be London-based although the office remained in Liverpool until 1938. Iberian was operated independently and their office had moved to London in 1936.

This growth was interrupted by the war in which he served with distinction in the army as an Embarkation Officer, rising to the rank of Captain - *"nothing heroic, just doing what he did best - organising moving people"*. Like Alec Hartwell, the country made the best use of his talents.

Blue Cars' operations restarted in 1946, contracting with coach companies in Italy, France and Switzerland to provide coaches in Blue Cars livery and to Ted Langton's specifications but still using the train or a hired coach to the cross-channel ferry. Thinking more widely, in 1948 he saw an opportunity to provide tours of England and Europe from the United States.

A 42-day European package for American tourists was introduced in May 1948 with Leslie Harris Travel of Dublin arranging the section in Eire. Approval was given by the Irish authorities and Blue Cars obtained six new Bedford OB chassis which were bodied by G J Roberts of Dublin. It then appears that this approval had been a mistake. The Eire section of the tour had to be abandoned and the unused coaches passed to Irish national transport operator CIE, which used them on the Dublin airport service.

"Only the best".
These pages from Blue Cars' 1949 brochure show the extensive tour network across Europe.

Ted Langton took great pride in his firm's brochures. Designing them himself, he would spend hours working on them and adjusting their design until he felt they were perfect.

PETER TULLOCH COLLECTION

Blue Cars required coaches hired on the continent for the season to be in Blue Cars livery. Here are French and Swiss coaches from 1948 and 1949.

PETER TULLOCH COLLECTION

Wartime restrictions on paper and colour printing were still in evidence in the April 1949 Blue Cars trade advertisement on the opposite page. Since it started in the 1930s, Blue Cars had owned no vehicles for its continental tours, preferring to hire coaches for a full season from operators on the continent. One condition of the hire was that the coaches were finished in Blue Cars colours and carried the firm's name.

PETER TULLOCH COLLECTION

A 1948 plan to operate Blue Cars tours in Eire in conjunction with Leslie Harris Travel of Dublin was at first approved by the Irish authorities, and Blue Cars bought six Bedford OBs with bodies by Roberts of Grangegorman, Dublin.

It seems this approval had been a mistake; the plan had to be cancelled and the unused coaches were bought by CIE, which used them on the Dublin airport service, as seen above.

CYRIL McINTYRE COLLECTION

Morris Commercial PVX 363, at the bottom of both of these pages, had one of the two coach bodies built by Page of Colchester - the Morris Commercial dealer which supplied the chassis and to whom Iberian's manager (G Page) was almost certainly related. The body looked not quite right.

In these pictures it's in London when new, loading passengers for Switzerland. There was not much up-market feel about the loading point at Kings Cross.

NA3T/A HUSTWITT

Scarborough-based Plaxton took the picture at the top of the opposite page is of four of the Morris Commercials on the Marine Drive in the town before delivery.

**PLAXTON ARCHIVE
at the KITHEAD TRUST**

Iberian had owned some coaches, the coach going with the passengers on the ferry, and a new fleet was needed when its tours restarted in 1950. In the immediate post-war years coaches ferried across the channel were subject to weather and tidal conditions and on some vessels a length or weight limit. Smith's and other operators were successfully operating continental tours with full-sized AECs and Leylands but use of smaller coaches gave more choice of route and flexibility of crossing time.

Always keen to provide the very best facilities for his clients, Ted Langton had little interest in engineering matters and this, perhaps, showed when late in 1949 Blue Cars ordered a fleet of thirteen Morris Commercial coaches for Iberian's operations. Well known for trucks and vans, Morris Commercial was not a name normally associated with the bus and coach industry and its newly introduced OP (diesel) and PP (petrol) were a late attempt to break into the Bedford-dominated lightweight coach market. It proved unsuccessful, being withdrawn from the market after two years of poor sales. However, it was forward-control with a full-width front and could be fitted with a body with no bulkhead behind the driver, like Beccols' Roadmaster, giving passengers an improved view of the continental scenery which they had paid to admire - and that was what was important to Ted Langton.

Twelve had Plaxton bodies and the other was bodied by Morris Commercial dealer and vehicle body builder Page of Colchester, which built only one other coach body and also one bus body - both on Morris Commercial chassis. Although the Plaxton-bodied ones were registered in Birmingham by Morris Commercial or its distributor, they were supplied through Page and this seems to have been a further reason for choosing the Morris Commercials, for at this time one G Page was Iberian's manager. Almost certainly a relation of the owners of the Colchester firm, he would have got Ted Langton a good deal.

Iberian's 1950 tours brochure featured the new Plaxton-bodied Morris fleet, which it described as Pullmans, although their noisy diesel engines rather spoiled this image.

Blue Cars and Iberian referred to their drivers as chauffeurs. The images of the coach were actually taken from one of a Plaxton-bodied Seddon, amended by hand to look something like one of the Morris Commercials.

PETER TULLOCH COLLECTION

The price of 85 guineas (a guinea was 105p) was about £2,700 at 2011 money values - much the same as a week's liner cruise or a five star week's air holiday in 2011.

PETER TULLOCH COLLECTION

Finished in a blue and silver livery similar to that of Blue Cars, the Morris Commercials had a 4.2-litre 6-cylinder diesel engine and a two-speed transfer box in addition to the usual four-speed gearbox - a transmission arrangement more familiar on military vehicles at the time. Far too rough and noisy for luxury continental touring, the diesel engines soon had to be replaced by the Morris four-cylinder 3,770cc 80bhp side-valve petrol engine, retaining the two gearboxes. Of a design well out of date, this engine was not the most spectacular of performers and, almost inevitably, proved underpowered, especially in the Alpine passes. An additional 20-gallon fuel tank (one nearside and one offside) was fitted to give an extended operating range.

Blue Cars decided to absorb Iberian at the end of the 1950 season and replace the Morrises with a new fleet of full-size coaches. When the government somewhat suddenly approved the general use of 30ft-long and 8ft-wide coaches in mid-1950, Blue Cars swiftly ordered twelve of the newly-announced Leyland Royal Tiger chassis, specifying uprated O.600 engines governed at 2,000 rather than the usual 1,800 rpm and high-ratio rear axles, giving a maximum road speed of 70 mph - drivers subsequently complained that whilst they went well enough, their brakes were not sufficiently powerful to stop the 8-ton coaches safely at these higher speeds.

The firm's publicity and tour brochures for the 1951 season emphasised the fleet being completely renewed and strengthened by the addition of the Leylands and new hired-in fleets in France and Italy. There would be a total of 36 owned and hired coaches against a vehicle requirement of around 30, thus allowing for duplication should a tour prove particularly popular and cover in case of accidents or breakdowns.

Subsequent publicity went on to declare that the new, larger luxury coaches would attract many tourists from the United States and Canada, announcing that the first had already departed on a three-month promotional tour of those countries from October 1950.

As if all this was not enough, the firm was also planning to provide luxury transport for affluent overseas visitors to the 1951 Festival of Britain.

Ted Langton was a trifle optimistic in making these announcements - he wanted luxurious bodies built to his own specification. Although orders for new buses and coaches were falling, all the big and most of the smaller coachbuilders were neither interested nor willing to build specials. The more so in this case for he had a considerable reputation for negotiating a keen price from his suppliers and then demanding more at that price. He had to find someone who would not only do a special design on time but also to his standards. Almost certainly he would have seen Smith's award-winning Roadmaster coach and been impressed with the excellent visibility it offered to its passengers, added to which was Beccols' willingness to do custom work. In July 1950 he phoned Westhoughton 2222.

The brochure shows the original intention was to have the same body on all 12 Royal Tigers.

Said to be inspired by American coach designs, the Beccols body looked striking and well proportioned, offering excellent all round visibility.

In the event there never was a Royal Tiger of this style finished in blue - the only one with the straight waist body was in the deep maroon St Christopher, New York, livery. The next five were blue but had the restyled body.

The seating on all six was reduced to 30.

The order for the final six was cancelled and they were bodied by Bellhouse Hartwell.

PETER TULLOCH COLLECTION

chapter 7
Success & disaster

The events of this chapter need a background of what was happening in the bus manufacturing industry, especially in regard to coaches. The post-war boom had come to an end and orders for the 1951 season were half the 1949 level. The big firms had surplus capacity and aggressively sought orders for their standard products. This made life even more difficult for the smaller firms and many gave up building coaches or went out of business.

The type of coach also changed. The 41-seat 30ft-long underfloor-engined coach made heavyweight forward-engined ones, such as Leyland's PS1 and PS2 or AEC's Regal III, obsolete overnight whilst the lighter forward-engined Bedford SB not only did away with the market for 29-seat normal-control coaches but, and equally importantly, provided a good lower cost solution for anyone that wanted a 33-seater. From a design point of view, Burlingham's stylish Seagull body took market share from everyone, including market-leader Duple which was building around 1,000 bodies a year.

Beccols was hit particularly hard. Thanks to the award-winning Roadmaster its 1950 season order level had been better than most, but all of the Roadmaster's special features were now provided as standard in an underfloor-engined coach. In 1950 Beccols built 32 Roadmasters, in 1951 it would build only 8.

With its principal design made obsolete overnight, Beccols not only needed work but also to establish itself as a credible supplier of stylish coach bodies for underfloor-engined chassis. Blue Cars order for twelve specially-designed luxury bodies was exactly what the firm needed. It was by far Beccols' biggest-ever order and the firm should, perhaps, have sought advice about dealing with a customer like Ted Langton.

Beccols simply got on with the job. George Nichols did the design and materials and parts were purchased for all twelve bodies. The first chassis was delivered early so that it could be bodied for the tour of the United States and Canada. After some hard work and very long hours at Norris Road, it was ready on time and finished to a very high standard.

Beccols promised Blue Cars a special luxury design - something which other coachbuilders would not do. After some very long hours at Norris Road, the first Royal Tiger was finished to a high standard and on time for the American tour. With its straight waistrail and roofline, said to be modelled on American Greyhound styling, the body was to be unique, as you can see at the top of this page. It was striking, distinctive and looked right - and Beccols was rightly proud of it.

In mid-October 1950, just before the coach left for Salford Docks to be loaded on to Manchester Liners' transatlantic service, the Beccols team proudly posed for this picture on the right.

Bert Beckett and George Nichols are on the left. Sadly, the smiles would soon fade and in less than a year most of them would be made redundant.

NICHOLLS ARCHIVE

The coach looked good with its assertive and striking straight waist rail and roof line modelled at Blue Cars' request on the styling of American Greyhound coaches. Lettered for Blue Cars' associate the New York-based St Christopher Travel Service of 30 Fifth Avenue, New York - a name better known in the United States than that of Blue Cars - its livery was not blue but a rich deep maroon with opulent-looking gold anodised trim. In mid-October 1950 the coach, later registered LYL 721, left Salford Docks for New York on a Manchester Liners cargo vessel. There was much publicity for both the tour and the new coach fleet which were dubbed 'wonder coaches' in the trade press. Bookings were high and the arrival of the remainder was awaited with great anticipation by the travel industry.

The cost must have been well beyond what Beccols had quoted but George Nichols and Bert Beckett were probably confident that Blue Cars appreciated what they had achieved and that the extra costs would be met. Leyland built the other eleven Royal Tiger chassis in October 1950 and five were delivered to Beccols in November, the rest were stored at Leyland.

Things then started to go wrong for Blue Cars. First the authorities refused permission to use 8ft-wide coaches in essential parts of central London. An attempt to get the decision reversed might take months and Blue Cars needed to protect its business. Nothing could be done about the 8ft-wide Royal Tiger chassis and it decided to retain the Morrises for another season and do something to improve their performance and appearance.

The first step was to fit Morris's new six-cylinder overhead-valve 4,197cc petrol engine, introduced late in 1950. This was physically longer, requiring modification to the front end of the body which gave an opportunity to fit a new, modern-looking front and windows in the front dome to improve passengers' forward vision. In this way they might seem more like the splendid new coaches Blue Cars had promised its clients. In retrospect Blue Cars should have hung on for approval of the 8-footers.

examples of bus & coach body production 1949-1951

	1949	1950	1951
Burlingham	530	460	255
Plaxton	335	255	240
Crossley	367	285	101
Roe	260	280	130
East Lancs	210	190	90
Harrington	190	175	90
Northern Counties	130	90	70
Massey	98	45	11
Bellhouse Hartwell	73	51	36
Yeates	70	65	45
Beccols	40	35	20

The coach's livery was not blue but a rich deep maroon with opulent-looking gold anodised trim and lettered for Blue Cars' associated New York-based St Christopher Travel Service of 30 Fifth Avenue, New York - a name better known in the United States than Blue Cars.

The coach was not registered when it went to the United States and Beccols took the opportunity to use the numberplate space for a small advertisement.

NICHOLLS ARCHIVE

Blue Cars decided to change the design of the rest of the Royal Tiger bodies to something with a curved roof and window line.

George Nichols had already done a design and it was in build on Leyland Royal Tiger chassis for local firms. In the pictures on this page you can see

MTE 550 for Progress of Chorley in the upper one, and MTF 298 for Monks of Leigh in the lower one.

With its bulbous front, the result was less than attractive.

NA3TA/HUSTWITT

Giving the job to Beccols was an easy decision - it had already built two Roadmaster bodies on Morris Commercial chassis. Fitting a Roadmaster front to the existing Plaxton body was not difficult but the work had to be done quickly and the bodies for the Royal Tigers were put on hold.

Blue Cars then seems to have changed its mind about the Royal Tiger coaches' styling - concerns appear to have arisen during the American tour. A more curvaceous approach was becoming fashionable for cars and coaches; straight lines were increasingly perceived as having undertones of wartime austerity. Although most United Kingdom coach builders were struggling to produce a good-looking underfloor-engined coach, especially in front-end appearance, all the designs featured curved styling.

With work on the Royal Tigers stopped, Blue Cars presumably saw no problem in asking that the design be changed. A bigger or stronger-minded coachbuilder (such as Alec Hartwell) would either have told Blue Cars what to do with its request or quoted a very high price and timescale for the alterations. Being dependent on the work, Beccols seems to have had little choice but to agree.

George Nichols had already produced "curved" designs and three bodies were in work for local operators. Royal Tigers MTE 550 for Progress, Chorley, and MTF 298 for Monks, Leigh, were the first but their front end looked uncomfortable. Much better-looking was Royal Tiger MTE 837 for Taylor, Earlestown, and it seems to have pleased Blue Cars. The materials bought and parts made for the straight line design had to be used with the result that whilst Beccols' standard design, as on MTE 837, had sloping body pillars, the revised Blue Cars bodies had the vertical pillars, rear end and other features of the original body.

A redesign produced something rather more stylish. The first example of this restyle to be completed was MTE 837, a Royal Tiger for Taylor of Earlestown, Newton-le-Willows.

This was accepted for the basis of the Blue Cars version, which would be slightly different, having to use the body frames already manufactured.

NICHOLLS ARCHIVE

Styling is subjective and fashion transient but in retrospect it is hard to make any judgement other than that the new version had neither the flair nor the presence of the original. Blue Cars' 1951 brochure, issued late in 1950, had made much of the introduction of the twelve new Royal Tigers with their specially-designed body but a 1951 press release highlighted the change and "improved design".

Beccols' founders, both basically coachbuilders, probably did not carefully estimate the impact all this would have on costs - they were used to supplying one or maybe two coaches to coach operators they knew well. More worrying was the effect on the firm's bank balance. Money spent on the parts for the Royal Tiger bodies would be "tied up" for several months until they were built and extra money had to be found for parts and materials for the Morris rebuilds. Cash became short and Beccols' suppliers started to ask for payment of their unpaid bills. There was little Beccols could do but press on and hope it all worked out.

Things got worse when Blue Cars' decision to give priority to the Morrises and postpone the Royal Tigers turned out to be a bad one. Most of the restrictions on use of 8ft-wide coaches in central London were suddenly removed at the end of March 1951, in time for the start of the tours season and the politically sensitive May opening of the Festival of Britain.

Beccols was on the receiving end. In addition to the Morrises Blue Cars now wanted the eleven Royal Tigers quickly and put pressure on Beccols. Besides cash, the restricted space in the Norris Road huts was a serious problem. It became clear that the Royal Tigers were going to be late - one would be ready for April with four more for June but the other six could not be completed until at least the second half of Blue Cars' season. With its tours fully booked and considerable extra work for the Festival of Britain, Blue Cars would have to hire some high quality coaches to cover their work and this would be expensive.

This, however, was nothing compared to the impact on Blue Cars' (and Ted Langton's) reputation in the market, for much had been made of the new specially-designed luxury fleet not only in England but also in Europe and the United States. Like Alec Hartwell, Ted Langton was not tolerant of anyone who let him down and his personal standing and reputation in the market was likely to be badly damaged. He refused to pay Beccols.

Try as it might Beccols could not get any payment from Blue Cars. The sum owing was more than one third of a year's turnover and supporting that shortfall was beyond its financial resources. With its mainly local market of trusted family firms, many of whom were personal friends, it had never needed extended banking facilities. Now Beccols desperately needed to pay its various bills.

With Beccols refusing (and probably unable) to do more work until Blue Cars paid, the contract appears to have been terminated. By July 1951 the firm was in financial trouble; most of the staff were laid off.

Blue Cars now needed to find someone who could be relied upon to body the remaining Royal Tigers to its specification in good time for the start of the 1952 season. This time it would not be easy. True that there was a drop in demand but in such circumstances coachbuilders looked after their existing clients and Blue Cars would have to take its place at the end of their production schedule. Its treatment of Beccols would be on the industry grapevine - whoever took on the job would be extra cautious.

With hindsight one can see that, in a brave attempt to sustain its business in a falling market, Beccols' owners had taken on two prestigious but high risk orders which were too large for their financial resources and from a client in whom they placed too much trust. They were used to dealing with clients with whom there was a great deal of mutual respect - a word at the lodge, Rotary Club, or Saturday's

When Blue Cars was refused permission for use of 8ft-wide coaches in important areas of London it decided to retain and improve the Morrises with a new engine and new front.

On the left you can see KOE 203 still waiting for its Blue Cars emblem and new rear glass to be fitted when Beccols took the formal pictures. It even had the stickers left from its last tour in the rear window.

The Beccols front was blended neatly with the Plaxton body and the result looked like a complete design, not something tacked on to the front.

The words FUEL OIL above the filler are a painter's error.

The seats and view to the rear, shown on the opposite page, were entirely Plaxton. The courier's seat to the left of the driver was able to swivel round so that the courier could face the passengers whilst speaking through the microphone.

NICHOLLS ARCHIVE

Ted Langton

There are few pictures of the completed Morris rebuilds in service with Blue Cars. On the right is KOE 207 in London.

ROY MARSHALL

Below, beginning to look its age, is Beccols' first Royal Tiger, MTE 550, still with original owner (Progress of Chorley) in 1964.

GEOFF LUMB

rugby match would ensure fair treatment. Dealing with an entrepreneur such as Ted Langton needed a much harder approach.

The rights and wrongs of disputes are never easy. Facts, as opposed to emotions, are always scarce but with hindsight Blue Cars' treatment of Beccols does seem harsh. What was yet more cruel was that the work went a mile down the road - to Bellhouse Hartwell.

The other full-size coaches in hand were two Royal Tigers - GET 601 for Billie's of Mexborough and GET 707 for Smart of Greasborough, both in Yorkshire, an Austin for Butterworth of Blackpool, two Regal IIIs for Florence/Kia-Ora of Morecambe, a Regal IV for Wright of Newark and a rebodied pre-war Leyland for local operator Sharrock. On the right is a somewhat battered GET 707 when with Garner of Bridge of Weir in June 1963.

J S COCKSHOTT ARCHIVE

This is LYL 722 on the left outside Blue Cars' head office in Shaftesbury Avenue, London. Iberian's office was to the left, behind the coach.

V JONES

Evidence of the pressure on Beccols is in this official picture. The coach is uncompleted - it has no seats and the rear glass screen is missing with its interior loose. Even the photography was not brilliant. To cover the delay in delivery and lack of the other six, Blue Cars had to hire coaches at high cost; the damage to its reputation in the market was great. Not tolerant of those who let him down, Ted Langton refused to pay Beccols.

NICHOLS ARCHIVE

The revised Blue Cars design used the body frames already in work and combined the vertical body pillars and rear end styling of LYL 721 with a gently curved window line. Somehow the result did not look as impressive as LYL 721 but in 1951 it was undoubtedly more fashionable.

ROY MARSHALL

chapter 8

Re-enter Alec Hartwell

The six Landmasters, MLF 341-46, were delivered promptly - the first going to the January 1952 Salon de l'Automobile show in Brussels. It and four more were licensed in February 1952 with the sixth held back until the season started in April.

The side trim design was revised for Blue Cars, as you can see in the picture on this page. Known as the Landmaster Mark III, the polished aluminium horizontal striping was fairly blatantly copied from Sheffield United's fleet.

BELLHOUSE HARTWELL ARCHIVE

Bellhouse Hartwell did some trading in coaches part exchanged for new ones and advertised the Beccols-bodied Royal Tigers and the Morris Commercials in Commercial Motor in September and October 1951, shown at the top of the opposite page.

This seems to have been somewhat speculative, as they were still in use. In the event Blue Cars kept the Morrises for a further season.

LYL 721-25 went to Bellhouse Hartwell client Eddie Holden for his Shaw and Spencer fleets. He ran them for a single season and they then passed to substantial lives with other operators who probably had no idea of their history. LYL 726 passed to Blankley, (Gem) of Colsterworth in Lincolnshire.

In the second column of the advert, the 1949 Bellhouse Hartwell-bodied Crossley offered for sale (by Margo of Bexleyheath) was EN 9535, which had been new to Auty of Bury.

Bellhouse Hartwell had a very stylish, modern, metal-framed design for which it had a stock of parts and sub-assemblies ready in its stores plus the capacity to do the work in the required timescale and a reputation for high quality. It agreed to supply Landmaster bodies for the six remaining Royal Tiger chassis with an option on a further 12.

This time, however, one tough and successful entrepreneur was dealing with another. There would be no question of special designs or any work without bank-guaranteed payments. The Landmaster design was only slightly modified for Blue Cars - known as the Mark III, the principal change was cosmetic external embellishments. Ben Goodfellow, general manager of Sheffield United, would have been flattered by the styling of the side flash with its horizontal strips of polished aluminium which originated with his firm. The first was photographed complete in November 1951 and exhibited at the January 1952 Brussels Salon de l'Automobile show from which the respected journal Bus and Coach reported with approval that, *"very dignified it looked when compared with some of its rather flashy Belgian contemporaries ..."*. The rest were delivered on time early in 1952 - and paid for on delivery.

For reasons which are not clear, Bellhouse Hartwell either took the six Beccols-bodied Royal Tigers in part exchange or sold them on behalf of one or other of the parties in the dispute. Although they remained in service with Blue Cars until the end of October 1951, in the previous month Bellhouse Hartwell was already advertising them and the Morrises for sale, offering to re-seat the Royal Tigers to 41 or the Morrises to 30. Five of the Royal Tigers were sold to Bellhouse Hartwell client Oldham-based Eddie Holden, LYL 722-23 went to his Stanley Spencer fleet and LYL 721/24-25 to his T Shaw and Son subsidiary. Holden ran them for a season after which they had substantial lives with other operators who probably had no idea of their history, most running until 1963/4. The sixth went to Blankley of Colsterworth, Lincs. The Morrises stayed with Blue Cars for the 1952 season being needed for the tours which went via Harwich, on the route to which a width restriction remained in force for some time.

As with all advanced designs there were a few in-service problems with the Landmasters. The large windscreen area suffered from water leaks. Similar problems were experienced on bodies built by much larger firms - Leyland's coach body for the Royal Tiger could suffer from copious leaks from its complex metal-framed front and side windscreen window frames. A more unusual problem with the Landmaster was trouble in opening and closing the passenger doors in the high summer temperatures of southern Europe, the cause being differential expansion of the body and door frames in the heat. Bellhouse Hartwell quickly resolved them all and Blue Cars was very satisfied with its Landmasters.

MLF 341-46 were fitted out to Bellhouse Hartwell's usual high standards using quality materials and much attention to detail. The offside emergency exit door was fitted with built-in steps for use on the continent.

BELLHOUSE HARTWELL ARCHIVE

Two more Royal Tiger
Landmasters (MXV 347/48)
joined the Blue Cars fleet in 1952.
They looked the same as the MLF batch.
Blue Cars sold them to dealer Frank Cowley
in January 1960 and they went on to
substantial lives with subsequent operators.

MXV 348 was bought by Edward Heyes of
St Helens in January 1960. Here it is above
in April 1961, by which time it had had
some alterations to stop rain ingress
through the fresh air intakes above the
windscreen. Heyes ran it until July 1963.

BELLHOUSE HARTWELL ARCHIVE

The choice of chassis
for the additional Landmasters showed that
Ted Langton was still after a good deal. There were three more
on Royal Tiger chassis, one of which was left-hand drive and 33-ft long, being
a cancelled order for Brazil. Then came a Sentinel, also 33ft-long and left-hand drive
it had been ordered by a firm called Drake Expeditions for tours in Argentina.
These came to nothing and Blue Cars bought the chassis, presumably at a knock
down price. Normally kept on the continent, the two 33-footers needed special
permission to run in England. Another Sentinel followed - it had been exhibited by
Sentinel at the 1952 Commercial Motor Show in the livery of
Smith's of Wigan. Daimler's Freeline underfloor-engined
chassis was never popular in the United Kingdom although
it sold well enough overseas and when fitted with Daimler's
10-litre engine was powerful and very smooth running.
Ted Langton bought eight. There was almost certainly an
advantageous deal in all of these purchases.

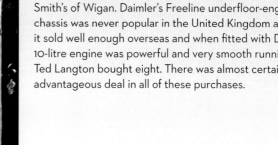

One reason Bellhouse Hartwell could offer quick delivery was
that it had already made parts for a production run of 20 or
more Landmasters. The Royal Tiger chassis were in store at
Leyland and all that had to be done was to assemble the
bodies and trim them to Blue Cars' specification. This picture
shows Landmaster parts in the stores at Greenvale.

BELLHOUSE HARTWELL ARCHIVE

Alec Hartwell lost no time in getting some publicity from the deal. The correspondent from Coaching Journal was clearly impressed with his visit to Greenvale, although his forecast that the company had a big future in the industry was not quite right. Bellhouse Hartwell did indeed have a big future - in aircraft and aerospace.

PETER TULLOCH COLLECTION

The Landmaster styling was slightly updated for this Sentinel. Below is Alan Lee's design sketch.

ALAN LEE

A feature of Blue Cars Continental tours is that the operator provides each passenger with a suitcase, which becomes his own property at the end of the tour. The rear luggage locker is, therefore, designed to accommodate thirty-four standard cases, which includes, of course, the driver's and courier's luggage. Additional locker space is available on the offside of the vehicle, which will accommodate a reasonable quantity of luggage and a separate compartment is also available for the tool kit.

I have described this body in some detail as it represents the latest production of the Bellhouse, Hartwell concern and is of particular interest at this time when plans for the 1952 season are on the point of completion by operators all over the country. It should be borne in mind, however, that, basically, this particular coach is identical with other productions from the Westhoughton factory and that other coaches by this builder are equally notable for their sturdy construction, attractive design and high quality of the detail work which can do so much to make or mar a passenger's comfort on long-distance journeys by road.

Amongst well-known operators who have found "Landmaster" bodies highly satisfactory from all points of view are Scout Motor Services, who use them on the Blackpool–London service; Transglobe Tours, of Birmingham; Knowles, of Bolton; Melba Motors, of Stockport; and Bury's, of Taunton. Chassis used for these operators include the Leyland "Royal Tiger", A.E.C., Regal Mark IV, and the Foden.

The "Monarch" coach for forward-control chassis has been supplied to numerous operators, including Embankment Motors, of Plymouth, on Maudslay chassis, and the Newquay Motor Co., on Tilling-Stevens chassis. The special Fordson coaches, too, have been in considerable demand.

When I visited the Westhoughton works and was shown round by Mr. A. W. Hartwell, I was impressed with the facilities available for body construction. The works are very fully equipped and, apart from coach bodies, the company manufactures a variety of aircraft components as well as aluminium hollow-ware and other products which call for a high standard of precision engineering. This long experience in precision engineering is clearly reflected in the design and construction of Bellhouse, Hartwell coaches, and the company has, undoubtedly, a big future in this industry.

Reprinted from

The Coaching Journal and Bus Review

December, 1951

With the Compliments of:

Bellhouse, Hartwell & Co., Ltd.,
Green Vale Works,
Westhoughton,
Lancs.

PRINTED BY W. P. GRIFFITH & SONS, LTD., LONDON AND BEDFORD.

For the 1952 Commercial Motor Show the Landmaster's front end styling was revised, and the result was called the Landmaster Mark IV. The first was a Sentinel in Smith's, Wigan livery.

It did not go to Smith's, however, but was bought by Blue Cars where it became NLR 850. It was repainted and the Blue Cars side trim added,

BELLHOUSE HARTWELL ARCHIVE

Another Sentinel, MYV 637, was an opportunistic purchase by Blue Cars. The 33ft-long and left-hand drive chassis had been ordered by an English firm, Drake Expeditions, for use on proposed tours of Patagonia from a Buenos Aires, Argentina, base.

They did not materialise, so Ted Langton bought it and sent it to Greenvale for a body. It was on Bellhouse Hartwell's stand at the 1952 Motor Show, complete with a Blue Cars hostess. 33ft-long coaches were not generally permitted in the United Kingdom and MYV 637, together with the other 33-footer MXV 440, were based in Ostend, their infrequent visits to England requiring a special permit specifying the precise roads to be used.

Do not be misled by the picture - the coach is left-hand drive and the main passenger door was on the other side of the coach and in the centre. In contrast to NLR 850 it had a lavatory and a buffet compartment.

BELLHOUSE HARTWELL ARCHIVE

This is NLR 850 having just been delivered to Blue Cars. The front nearside pair of seats by the driver was removed and replaced by a courier seat which, legally, would not be available for passenger use. The picture shows the kitchen/ buffet (but no lavatory) area at the back of the coach

BELLHOUSE HARTWELL ARCHIVE

Completely bizarre was an order for six small lightweight Dennis Stork chassis. Powered by a 4-cylinder underfloor-mounted engine, the Stork was generally intended for van and pantechnicon use. A few were bodied as basic school buses for use in London. There is no record of whose bodies these might have had but it was an odd choice for luxury coach work and the order has echoes of the Morris Commercials.

The Storks never arrived. On 20th April 1953 Ted Langton sold Blue Cars (Continental) Ltd for £126,000 to the British Electric Traction group (BET), owner of the majority of the United Kingdom's privately-owned buses and coaches, including such well-known fleets as Ribble, Southdown and Midland Red. The deal included the licences, goodwill and assets of two other Langton tour firms - Luxury Land Cruises Ltd and Continental Land Cruises Ltd. Ted Langton retained and later reused the names. The BET formed Blue Cars Continental Coach Cruises Limited to acquire the businesses, including the fleet of Landmasters (Royal Tigers MLF 341-46 and MXV 347/48, left-hand drive MXV 440 and Sentinels MYV 637 and NLR 850). Daimlers NLR 711-16, 848-49 were delivered to the BET, which cancelled the Storks at once.

Blue Cars' next order was for eight more Landmasters, this time on Daimler Freeline chassis with smooth running Daimler engines.

By the time the coaches entered service Ted Langton had sold Blue Cars to the BET group. Registered NLR 711-16, 848/49 they were delivered during 1953, the last not being licensed until 1954, having been used for brake development work by Lockheed.

NLR 849, shown below, still carries the Blue Cars name on its front but had passed to Shaw, Bolton when it took part in the first North West Coach Rally in April 1960. Specially trimmed with then fashionable white wall tyres, the Daimler leaves Wigan market place for Blackpool. It rained.

J S COCKSHOTT ARCHIVE

Next were three Leyland Tiger Cubs, OLL 946-48. The heavy-frame chassis were part of an order for 28 export model OPSUC1/1 bus chassis from Leyland's associate DAB, Denmark which had been reduced to 19.

The BET bought three of the surplus ones for Blue Cars, but had Leyland modify the chassis to resemble the home market PSUC1/2 coach chassis by fitting a rear drop-frame extension. Here is the last of the three in the overflow park at London's Victoria Coach Station.

J S COCKSHOTT ARCHIVE

Bellhouse Hartwell came close to its hoped-for big company sales when it won follow-on orders from the BET group for three Landmaster bodies for Blue Cars, and then eight more. "The bodies were offered at a very competitive price such that we couldn't really refuse" - whether this was a case of Alec Hartwell trying to buy into a market or disposing of surplus material stocks is unclear for by that time the coach market was even more difficult. The eight were allocated to Blue Cars (6) and Hebble (2) on Royal Tiger chassis and then reassigned to Blue Cars (2), Hebble (4) and two on AEC Reliance chassis for Sheffield United.

Alec Hartwell then gained orders for eight Landmasters from the BET group - something he had always wanted to achieve, hoping it might lead to more. *"The bodies were offered at a very competitive price such that we couldn't really refuse"*. If the order turned into bigger things that would be good, but if, as was the case, the major coachbuilders continued to dominate the BET's business, then it used up some of the stocks of parts in the Greenvale stores.

The coaches were allocated to Blue Cars (2), Hebble (4) and Sheffield United (2). Blue Cars' two were Leyland Royal Tigers PGK 473/74, new in October 1954. The rain shield, fitted across the top of the windscreen, gave the coach something of a frowning appearance. This picture on the left shows the pair in front of one of the Leyland Tiger Cubs.

ROY MARSHALL

Delivered in 1954, the Hebble vehicles, fleetnumbers 71-74, were also Leyland Royal Tigers (ECP 205/06, 499, 500). They were later renumbered 33-36.

J S COCKSHOTT ARCHIVE

Colour pictures of the Landmaster Mark IV are hard to find and ones in Blue Cars livery even more so. This somewhat blurry image of Leyland Tiger Cub OLL 948 was extracted from a still frame from a Blue Cars publicity film.

BET

Delivered in 1955, the two for Sheffield United were on AEC Reliance chassis. They were numbered 253 and 254. 254 is shown above and in colour below. It was almost at the end of its life with Sheffield United Tours in the colour shot, being sold in 1963.

J S COCKSHOTT ARCHIVE (upper)
PETER ROBERTS (lower)

On the left is Sheffield United Tours 253

J S COCKSHOTT ARCHIVE

Below are three of Hebble's four Landmasters, working a holiday excursion to Scarborough in 1962, parked alongside a Northern General Harrington Cavalier bodied Leyland Leopard.

PETER ROBERTS

(Above) One of Hebble Motor Services' new coaches. It has a 37-seater Land-master body by Bellhouse-Hartwell on a Royal Tiger chassis.

British body lines characterize the bodywork of this Blue Cars' coach which was built in Belgium by Ruysschaert Philippart.

BUS & COACH, SEPTEMBER 1954

Unexpected similarity

My attention has been drawn to the quite remarkable similarity in external appearance of four coaches recently taken into use by Hebble Motor Services Ltd. and eight others which Blue Cars Continental Coach Cruises Ltd. has had built in Belgium by Ruysschaert Philippart on Leyland Royal Tiger chassis for service on the Continent. It will be seen from the illustrations on page 318 that their resemblance is obvious.

The explanation is that Bellhouse, Hartwell and Co. Ltd., which is responsible for the Hebble coachwork, at one time also built some similar bodies for Blue Cars, and when it was decided to have the new ones constructed in Belgium it was agreed that they should be given the same external appearance as the earlier Bellhouse-Hartwell models. It would seem that the Belgian body-builder has done his work well.

In September 1954 the Hebble vehicles caught the attention of one of the correspondents to the respected monthly journal Bus and Coach.

After its sale to the BET, Blue Cars expanded its fleet of left-hand drive coaches on the continent. Built to the longer length permitted there, this included eight Leyland Royal Tigers delivered in 1954 with bodies by the Belgian coachbuilder Carrosserie H. Ruysschaert-Philippart, which were styled to look generally similar to the Landmasters. There was a considerable tax advantage in buying locally built bodies for continental use. Their front grilles almost certainly came from the Bellhouse Hartwell stores at Greenvale.

Built early in 1955 the two Landmaster bodies for Sheffield United plus one for small new independent operator Tartan Arrow Service were the last. Bellhouse Hartwell's involvement in coachbuilding was over, although the firm had stocks of parts for several more Landmasters which it kept for some years *"just in case"*.

In 1954 the BET bought eight left-hand drive Royal Tigers which, because of a favourable tax break, it had bodied by Belgian coachbuilder Carrosserie H Ruysschaert-Philippart. The contract specified that their styling should be based on that of the Landmaster and some parts including the front grille came from Bellhouse Hartwell.

However, for both Ted Langton and Alec Hartwell the future was in the skies.

There was one final Landmaster and it was an unusual purchase. London-based Tartan Arrow Service was a privately-owned removals and haulage firm and PYU 4 was its only coach.

New in July 1955, it ran on hire to Northern Roadways of Glasgow on the latter's London service. Severely damaged in an accident after a short time in service, in 1958 it was rebuilt as a van, still with Tartan Arrow. This admittedly poor picture is one of the very few of the coach in service

NA3T/A HUSTWITT

The Beccols-bodied Royal Tigers all went on to a succession of new owners, who probably had no idea of their complex history.

Above left is LYL 721 with Lander's of Rainworth, Notts, who ran it for over 10 years and held it in very high regard. It featured in Leyland adverts during 1960 and Mr Lander in praising it said *"…we have never had a vehicle to compare with this Royal Tiger…"*

UNKNOWN

At the bottom is LYL 723 with Lamcote Coaches of Radcliffe-on-Trent. Lamcote operated it from 1955 to 1963.

ROY MARSHALL

chapter 9
Beccols tries again

Having had to lay off most of its workforce, Beccols struggled on for a few months. The final body was completed in April 1952 just as the firm was placed in the hands of the liquidators. For Sharrock of Westhoughton, OTB 861, top right, was on a rebuilt pre-war Leyland TS chassis. Sharrock did several such rebuilds and the origin of this one and that of NTB 147 (pictured below), completed the previous June, remain a mystery.

R H G SIMPSON

Meantime, Beccols struggled on with a tiny workforce, completing three bodies in August 1951, one in September, another in December and one in April 1952. It was to no avail, the financial situation was hopeless and in February 1952, the firm's creditors petitioned for Beccols' insolvency. On 6th March the directors convened an Extraordinary General Meeting at which it was resolved *"That it has been proved to the satisfaction of this meeting that the Company cannot by reason of its liabilities continue its business, and that it is advisable to wind up the same, and accordingly that the Company be wound up voluntarily, and that Mr James Wood of 21 Mawdesley Street Bolton be and he is hereby appointed Liquidator for the purposes of such winding-up."*

Although Bert Beckett and his wife owned a thriving Bolton fish and chip shop, they had four school-age children to bring up and educate. It seems, too, that he had lost respect for his business partner. Bert Beckett therefore joined Plaxton's (Scarborough) Ltd, becoming their highly successful North-West area sales manager. Well respected and very much liked in the coach industry, he had a successful career with the company until he retired.

Beccols, however, was not finished. On 24th October 1952 George Nichols and his eldest son Brian set up Beccols (1952) Ltd, based in the sheds at Norris Road.

The plan was to build van bodies and undertake vehicle body repairs but by May 1953, having built a few 'Rivington' caravans, the new firm was insolvent. It was rescued by Maurice Edwards, the retired managing director of Bromilow and Edwards Ltd and his son-in-law John Briggs, who owned a coal merchant business.

Curiously, the new firm built some bus bodies but no coaches. The order came via the substantial Manchester-based Austin car dealers Syd Abrams Ltd for which Beccols had built commercial bodies. Abrams had contact with the Manchester branch of a French company which exported goods to West Africa. It somehow obtained an order for twelve (some accounts say eight) bus bodies on Austin chassis for export to Nigeria. Negotiations seem to have been started with either Beccols or Beccols (1952) - George Nichols' design and artist's impression of it is on Beccols paper and the order may have been the stimulus for Maurice Edwards' involvement. Some were built and shipped, although it is not clear how many were built, who bought and operated them, where or for what. No further orders were forthcoming.

the new
RIVINGTON
A magnificent 22ft. 4-berth model. Designed for year round Residence and Touring

BECCOLS · WESTHOUGHTON · LANCASHIRE · ENGLAND

In October 1952, seven months after Beccols went into liquidation, George Nichols and his eldest son Brian set up Beccols (1952) Ltd, based in the sheds at Norris Road to build van bodies and undertake vehicle body repairs.

However, the post-war boom was over and seven months later having built a few Rivington caravans and some commercial bodies, the new firm was insolvent. It was rescued by the retired managing director of Bromilow and Edwards Ltd.

NICHOLS ARCHIVE

Beccols (1952) built some buses but no coaches. Manchester-based Austin dealer, Syd Abrams Ltd, obtained a contract for 12 bodies on Austin chassis for export to Nigeria. Negotiations seem to have been started in 1952 as George Nichols' design impression is on Beccols paper, shown above. They were shipped in 1953 but it is not known how many were actually built - some reports give 8, others 12 - or for whom they ran.

NICHOLS ARCHIVE

There were further financial difficulties and in December 1954 the business and its assets were transferred to a new company, Hulton Products (Lancashire) Ltd owned jointly by Briggs and Edwards. Still based in the Norris Road huts, its stated aim was building commercial vehicle bodies and luxury caravans. Maurice Edwards was Managing Director. Neither of the Nichols was a director, George being employed as designer and works manager. Beccols (1952) Ltd became dormant but was not removed from the Register of Companies until 1963.

Hulton built one coach body. Completed in 1955 and designed by George Nichols, the coach was a rebody of a Leyland PS1/1 chassis for Sharp of Manchester. Thought by many to be one of the strangest-looking coaches ever, the result was named Tryphon and carried the equally bizarre title Sharps Stratocruiser.

Unhappy with the management and general direction of Hulton, both Nichols resigned in mid-1955. Brian Nichols started a vehicle body building business in Wigan. Initially this was too small to employ his father, who joined Crossley Motors, Errwood Park, Stockport, working in the body design office. Crossley was being slowly run down by the ACV Group and, after a year or so, aged 57 and tired of the long and difficult 70-mile round trip commute from his home at Upholland, George Nichols resigned and took a metal and woodwork teaching post at a school in Kirby, Liverpool.

Hulton recruited a new manager but by that time there were only five or six employees and the output of van and lorry bodies for local firms was tiny. It continued in this modest way until March 1971 when the firm was closed down, its few assets passing to Syd Abrams Ltd.

Brian Nichols' new business prospered, successfully moving out of vehicle bodies into shop and office fitting with premises in Chapel Lane, close to Wigan Corporation's Melverley Street bus garage. It grew quickly and George retired from teaching and joined his son, happily designing units and running the workshop into the 1980s. George Nichols died in March 1989. The shop-fitting company thrived, only being given up when Brian Nichols retired. Sadly, he passed away in November 2002, only a dozen or so years after his father.

One of the contributors to this book met George Nichols a couple of years before his death: *"It was a wonderful experience - a lovely man with a twinkle in his eye. I took all my Beccols pictures and some Bellhouse Hartwells too - he spotted the ringers straight away"*.

The Beccols (1952) business was transferred to a new firm, Hulton Products (Lancashire) Ltd, owned by Maurice Edwards and his son-in-law.

George and Brian Nichols were hired to run it. The Nichols father and son were unhappy with the new firm and resigned in 1955 but not before George Nichols produced his final design - the strange looking Tryphon. Typically bold and adventurous, it was out of line with current fashion.

Only one Tryphon was sold - a replacement body for a 1948 Leyland PS1 of Sharp's of Manchester, the original Pochin body of which had been condemned.

JNC 717 (in the pictures here it has an incorrect number plate - JMC 717) carried the name *Sharps Stratocruiser*, and was finished in red and metallic silver. Whilst the exterior looked strange, the interior styling was crisp and up-to-date. A unique vehicle, it ran until 1969.

NICHOLS ARCHIVE

chapter 10

Bellhouse Hartwell takes off

Aircraft sub-assembly work became the principal work at Greenvale, so much so that coachbuilding and hollowware were closed down. Below are wing fairings and engine doors for the Vickers VC10.

BELLHOUSE HARTWELL ARCHIVE

I n the 1950s there was huge growth in the high technology market for both military and civil aircraft with, in the case of defence work, attractive 'cost-plus' contracts. The demand for complex aircraft sub-assemblies burgeoned. The skills and quality control needed perfectly matched those of Bellhouse Hartwell with its reputation for careful high-class work.

No surprise that it attracted Alec Hartwell, who decided to concentrate on aerospace, withdrawing from hollowware and, more reluctantly, giving up coachbuilding. Orders were plentiful and a second company, Bellhouse Hartwell (Aerospace) Ltd, was registered in 1961. Greenvale Works was bought from the Bleachers Association in that year.

The company logo became a pair of stylised wings, surrounding the letters BHW which neatly captured the three key letters in the owners' surnames - BellHouse HartWell. Much later the letters from this logo - BHW - became the firm's name.

The two firms gained many contracts - for example, during the Korean War the Government ordered 1,000 Canberra reconnaissance planes and Bellhouse Hartwell secured a lucrative contract for the fuel tanks. It also made parts for the Lightning fighter and the AVRO 748. With the cyclical nature of the aircraft industry, the volume of work rose and fell in the 1960s and the size of the workforce varied accordingly.

In 1971, Alec Hartwell accepted a take-over offer from the growing aerospace group Hampson Industries Ltd, of Dudley; the Bellhouse Higson and Co textile business, still trading at a modest level, was closed down. As part of the take-over agreement, Alec remained as managing director until 1978 and during this time, when the business was in one of the aerospace industry's periodic recessions, made a buy-back offer to Hampson. It was declined.

Now part of a larger group, the firm grew, for example making parts for Canberra, Nimrod, Jaguar and VC10 aircraft. Greenvale was increasingly unsuitable for handling large sub-assemblies and housing modern computer-controlled machinery and in the late 1980s a new, modern factory was built at Caxton Close on the then new Wheatlea Industrial Estate in Wigan. Operated by a new company, BHW (Components) Ltd, it maintained the reputation for high quality, the workforce increasing to over 300. Greenvale works was closed on 18th July 2002.

The Hampson Group now has seven plants in England, seven in the United States and one in India; BHW Wigan is the headquarters of the Aerospace Fabrications and Assemblies Division. Its customers include Boeing, Airbus and Bombardier. BHW concentrates on sheet metal detail manufacture and sub-assembly airframe components, specialising in airframe component manufacture, fabricated new build structures and the repair/refurbishment of airframe assemblies on an extensive variety of aircraft ranging from Tornado to Airbus. At the time of writing, for example, it was building sub-assemblies for the Airbus A380 and Boeing 787.

The company holds the prestigious BAe Systems Supplier of Excellence Silver Award and is a holder of the North West Business Excellence Award. Its marketing strapline *Professionalism, Commitment and Excellence* well describes the company - it could equally be applied to its coachbuilding predecessor.

Left empty, almost inevitably Greenvale Works was set on fire by vandals on 28th October 2003. The site was then sold for housing development by Miller Homes in 2010, which renamed it Orchard Green. Greenvale House was converted to flats.

Having left Hampson, Alec Hartwell pursued other interests with typical flair and equal success. First was a printing company (Horcus Printing) in Burnley. Next, prompted by an interest in water gardening at his new home in Penn, Buckinghamshire, he opened a water-garden centre in the south of England and in

1969 started Lotus Water Garden Products Ltd, also based in Burnley. Both thrived and he commuted from Penn to Manchester in his private aircraft. Lotus made plastic-based parts for water gardening - pumps, liners and the like. Successful, it was sold for considerable gain in the 1990s to the Bunzl Group; later bought out, today it remains a major force in its industry.

Alec Hartwell died in 2002 - by then he also had houses in the South of France and the Cayman Islands. The following extract from the Lotus Water Garden Products web site perfectly captures that which drove him in his work: *"Lotus has been at the forefront of water garden product design for over thirty years. As the first company to introduce water gardening into the UK, we have been responsible for many major innovations and our expertise, reliability and reputation are unrivalled. Lotus brands are recognised worldwide and include Maximus and Olympus pumps, Toughline pools and the award winning Green Genie clear water systems."*

It ended with *"Innovation, Quality and Safety are the criteria by which all of our products are produced"*. For Alec Hartwell, they always had been.

Transporting aircraft parts required a long, low vehicle and Alec Hartwell acquired Leyland Tiger EK 8170 from Webster Bros of Wigan (owners of Smith's).

It had had an interesting life. New to Webster in 1931 it was originally a two-axle Leyland TS1 with a Burlingham body. Late in 1937 Webster had its chassis lengthened and a third trailing axle added. A Gardner 5LW engine replaced its petrol engine and the result was then rebodied by Santus.

It ran in this form, possibly being requisitioned for a time by the War Department, until the end of 1950 when Bellhouse Hartwell took it in part exchange for one of Smith's new coaches. Here it is above.

ROY MARSHALL

Greenvale then rebuilt it to a lorry with a smart new Landmaster-style cab, and it served as such from early 1952 to the end of 1956. Traded in for a new Bedford truck, it then passed to Hackett, Manchester for spares. On the left it is loaded with aircraft tail sections.

BELLHOUSE HARTWELL ARCHIVE

chapter 11

Blue Cars takes off

Euravia's first aircraft were three Lockheed Constellations bought from the Israeli airline El Al in 1962, followed by two more from Trans European including the one above, G-AHEN.

The airline's first flight was on 5th May 1962 from Manchester to Palma, Majorca. Ted Langton later retired to live in Palma.

ZOGGAVIA COLLECTION/ SCOTT HENDERSON

Having sold Blue Cars, in 1954 Ted Langton started Universal Sky Tours Ltd, usually known as Sky Tours, offering packaged holidays in Spain, Italy and the south of France with travel by air, contracting with hotels for rooms in bulk and insisting they provided things like en-suite facilities and swimming pools. He had invented the air package holiday and over the next ten years would develop the concept until it became a part of almost everyone's life - an achievement later recognised by the holiday travel industry.

In some aspects of this he fell foul of a covenant in the Blue Cars sale agreement preventing him from re-entering the coach tour business for seven years - a fairly normal piece of legal protection for the purchaser of an ongoing business. The BET duly took him to court and won the case in 1960, receiving damages of the then not inconsiderable sum of £45,000 - over one third of what it had paid for Blue Cars. By then he was well able to afford to pay - the Universal Sky Tours had indeed taken off and he dismissed the BET payment as *"a fleabite"*.

To carry passengers to their fortnight in the sun, Universal Sky Tours relied upon charter airlines. Most were small operations with elderly aircraft and Ted Langton was probably the first of many to be let down by cancellations leaving his clients stranded. When Falcon Airways and Air Safaris did just this by suddenly going out of business in 1961, his solution was brilliantly simple - he started his own airline.

Setting up an airline needed expert and experienced help - in licensing, engineering and the safe and reliable operation of a fleet of aircraft. He recruited J E D (Jed) Williams. Born in Liverpool, Jed Williams already had a distinguished academic, wartime and air industry track record. Cambridge graduate, aircraft

navigator with Argentine Airlines and then Chief Navigator with Israeli airline El Al, he had become Technical Adviser to the managing director of El Al. In 1959 he left to start an aircraft operation consultancy in which role he had begun to develop similar ideas to Ted Langton about vertically-integrated air holiday packages. He was exactly what Ted Langton needed to set up and manage the new airline. They got on well, their differing personalities complementing each other. Also from El Al as chief pilot came Derek Davison - a former El Al captain, previously a BOAC Comet first officer and before that an RAF bomber pilot.

Wholly owned by Universal Sky Tours, Euravia (London) Ltd was formed on 1st December 1961. The advent of jet airliners was making good reliable piston-engined aircraft available on the second-hand market and it was no surprise when Jed Williams bought three Lockheed Constellations (two L-049s and one L-149) from El Al, arranging for El Al to convert them to high density 82-seaters for Euravia.

The first flight, using Constellation G-ARVP, was from Manchester to Palma on 5th May 1962. It was, in retrospect, a memorable occasion - the first 'all from one company' package holiday flight. In October the operations and fleet of Skyways (three Lockheed L-749A Constellations and three AVRO Yorks) were taken over, although the deal did not include the Skyways Coach-Air cross-channel operation. During the winter two more L-049s were bought from Trans European.

Langton, Williams and Davison were a winning combination. The airline was well run, the package holiday business boomed and in 1964 six Bristol Britannia 175-102s were acquired from BOAC. On 16th August 1964 the airline's name was changed to Britannia Airways and the rest, as they say, is history.

In 1964 the Lockheeds were joined by six Bristol Britannia 175-102s from BOAC, and the airline's name was changed to Britannia Airways.

G-ANBA is seen below at Bristol Lulsgate September 1969.

CHRIS ENGLAND

The Universal Sky Tours and the airline were sold to the Thomson organisation in 1965, which quickly phased out the Constellations and then expanded operations with a fleet of Boeing 707 and 737 jets.

On the right is 737-204C G-AXNB on the approach to Dusseldorf in May 1982.

UDO HAAFKE

Boeing 757s and wide-body 767s followed. The fleet of 45 planes was all Boeings - 17 737s, 18 757s and 10 767s. 757-204 G-BYAX is on the opposite page at the top landing at Corfu in 2004.

Renamed Thomson Airways in 2005, it and Universal Sky Tours are now part of the German TUI group.

DANNY VERSTEEGEN

Taking off from where Euravia began. The main picture opposite shows 767-304 G-OBYF lifting off from a wet runway at Manchester in September 2004

DEREK MANNING

In 1965, following the pattern of Happiways and Blue Cars, Ted Langton sold Universal Sky Tours and Britannia Airways to the Thomson International organisation. The contract required that Ted Langton, Jed Williams and David Davison stay on and manage the operation for at least five years. Ted Langton found the new organisation difficult. Used to running his own show and taking all the decisions, the structured approach of managers and committees was not how he worked; both sides agreed to him leaving in 1967.

Britannia Airways then expanded quickly. One of their key moves was to buy a brand new fleet of Boeing jets. The business continued to grow rapidly and Britannia became the United Kingdom's second largest airline after British Airways with 45 Boeings - 17 737s, 18 757s and 10 767s. His contract completed, Jed Williams left in 1969 to pursue new ventures in aircraft finance and operations, moving to a farm in Tuscany. David Davison then took over, going on to become the highly successful Chief Executive until he retired in 1988, his experience and advice sought by governments and manufacturers on both sides of the Atlantic. Renamed Thomson Airways in 2005, it and Universal Sky Tours are now part of the German TUI group and few of its passengers know the origin of the airline on which they travel.

After some involvement in cruise holidays which ended with the 1972/3 oil crisis and with a continuing involvement in tours, in 1975 he retired to his house in Palma, Majorca - also buying a hotel there *"just to keep my hand in"*.

He left a legacy in the north-west - the Langton Adventure Centre in the Lake District. Established as a charitable trust in 1970, it is based in a lovely former farmhouse in the small hamlet of Hartsop, Cumbria, near the bottom of Kirkstone pass and close to Brotherswater. The purpose of the trust was for the centre "to be used as and for an adventure centre for character training to help boys, girls and young people through their leisure time activities so to develop their physical, mental and spiritual capacities that they may grow to full maturity as individuals and members of society...".

Ted Langton died in 1978, aged 74. His obituary noted that *"he invented and developed the packaged air holiday. Investing his own capital, he encouraged development of better hotels, with en-suite rooms and swimming pools, guaranteeing contracts for room booking with hotel owners"* and it was also said *"that where Ted Langton went, others followed"*. A truly exceptional man.

chapter 12

Production

These annual lists are in alphabetical order by operator, listed by the year in which the vehicle first ran in service with its Beccols or Bellhouse body. The lists have been kept simple, as details such as months first licensed, chassis and body numbers and subsequent owners will be found in other publications.

There are no company records of production for either firm. What's contained in these lists is the best information the authors have been able to assemble by reference to many sources. Where they are at variance with other previously published information, we believe this version to be the more accurate. The authors are aware of other vehicles sometimes shown as having bodies by one or other of the two firms - examples being AEC Regal HMX 987 and Leyland Tiger ATB 31 - all have been investigated and are believed wrongly attributed.

All the Commer Q4 chassis started life during the war as government lorries; sold as surplus they were converted for coach use by various dealers.

Bellhouse Hartwell Fordson bodies were of two types - long (up to 34 seats) and short (29 or 30 seats). These are indicated in the lists, noting that some of the long version had only 30 seats.

Body type and seating codes

F indicates a full-width front where this would not normally be fitted

C indicates coach - **RC** a raised rear section observation coach

B indicates bus

the numbers are the seating capacity excluding driver and courier's seats

the final **F** or **C** indicates front or centre entrance.

Several of the photographs in this section show coaches with their later owners.

year	Bellhouse	Beccols	Hulton
1938-9	**1** (or more?)	-	-
1947	**15**	**7**	-
1948	**47**	**21**	-
1949	**73**	**40**	-
1950	**51**	**35**	-
1951	**36**	**20**	-
1952	**27**	1	-
1953	**12**	**8** or **12**?	-
1954	**9**	-	-
1955	**4**	-	**1**

HTC 514
JP 6468 | JP 6323

reg no	chassis		body layout	supplied to	
FV 1902	Leyland Tiger TS3	ℝ	C32F	**Simpson** Manchester	new in 1931

one or maybe two more may have been in work

reg no	chassis		body layout	supplied to	
JP 1142	Leyland Tiger TS7	ℝ	C32F	**Liptrot** Bamfurlong	
BNE 577	Leyland Tiger TS7	ℝ	C32F	**Mayers** Liverpool	rejected at first due to tilt test failure; rear axle and wheels modified and then taken by Pownall;
CTF 167	Leyland Tiger TS8	ℝ	C32F	**Mayers** Liverpool	
JTB 20	Foden PVSC5		C33F	**Monks** Leigh	in 1949 to Thomson of Kirkwall, Orkney
◖ HTC 514	Thornycroft Nippy		C23F	**Pownall** Golborne	
◖ JP 6468	Leyland Tiger PS1/1		C33F	**Smith** Wigan	rebodied Harrington FC33F in 1953
JP 6569	AEC Regal I		C33F	**Smith** Wigan	

reg no	chassis		body layout	supplied to	
EK 8203	Leyland Tiger TS1	ℝ	C33F	**Abbott** Timperley	
CFV 36	Leyland Tiger PS1/1		C33F	**Lansdowne** Fleetwood	rebodied by KW Bodies FC33F by 1954
VU 3270	AEC Regal	ℝ	C33F	**Mills & Seddon** Farnworth	rebuilt with full front by Shutt of Burnley in 1954
HTF 617	Leyland Tiger PS1/1		C33F	**Morecambe Motors** Morecambe	rebodied by Harrington FC35F in 1952
DNE 338	Leyland Tiger TS7	ℝ	C33F	**Shaw** Oldham	
EBU 84	Leyland Tiger PS1/1		C33F	**Shaw** Oldham	
EBU 85	Leyland Tiger PS1/1		C33F	**Shaw** Oldham	
ADH 583	Leyland Tiger TS6	ℝ	C33F	**Smith** Wigan	rebodied by Harrington FC33F in 1953
JP 6469	Leyland Tiger PS1/1		C33F	**Smith** Wigan	
EBU 37	Leyland Tiger PS1/1		C33F	**Spencer** Oldham	body to AEC Regal APC 421 with Arscott of Chagford in 1956
RX 9307	Leyland Tiger TS4	ℝ	C33F	**Spencer** Oldham	
AG 8280	Leyland Tiger TS4	ℝ	C33F	**Webster** Wigan	lettered Smith of Wigan as legal owner
◖ JP 6323	Leyland Tiger PS1/1		C33F	**Webster** Wigan	
JP 6411	Leyland Tiger PS1/1		C33F	**Webster** Wigan	rebodied by Harrington FC37F and re-registered OMB 468 with Holt of Whitworth in 1952
KJ 5433	Leyland Tiger TS4	ℝ	C33F	**Webster** Wigan	

Some of these bodies carried Bellhouse Higson maker's transfers and, because of this, are recorded thus in some records. So far as can be established, only ADH 583 and AG 8280 were completed before the Bellhouse Hartwell company was formed.

ℝ rebodied

◖ photograph on opposite page

◖ photograph below

reg no	chassis	body layout	supplied to	
JTE 612	Commer Commando	C30F	**Bold** Melling	
CK 4315	Leyland Tiger TS2	® C33F	**Butterworth** Blackpool	
DBA 936	Commer Q4	® C30F	**Fieldsend** Salford	
JTJ 642	Commer Commando	C30F	**Harrison** Morecambe	
JP 7220	Austin K4/CXB	C30F	**Howarth** Westhoughton	
KTU 237	Leyland Tiger PS1/1	C33F	**K&S** Manchester	*rebodied by Duple FC35F in 1955 with Peascod of Liverpool*
CWH 510	AEC Regal III	C33F	**Knowles** Bolton	*rebodied by Duple FC35F in 1955 with Lloyd of Nuneaton*
JP 7066	Leyland Tiger PS1/1	C33F	**Liptrot** Bamfurlong	*rebodied by Harrington C35F in 1952; Beccols body to Austin of Stafford LRE 463*
JP 7067	Leyland Tiger PS1/1	C33F	**Liptrot** Bamfurlong	*rebodied by Harrington FC35F in 1953*
HTJ 637	Leyland Tiger PS1/1	C33F	**Mayers** Liverpool	*later rebuilt with full front*
JTE 970	Leyland Tiger PS1/1	C33F	**Mayers** Liverpool	
EUX 102	Commer Q4	® C33F	**Morris** Bridgnorth	
JTJ 270	Leyland Tiger PS1/1	C33F	**Poxon** Blackrod	
BWB 187	Leyland Tiger TS7	® C33F	**Progress** Chorley	
JP 2954	Leyland Tiger TS7	® C33F	**Progress** Chorley	
JP 6686	AEC Regal I	C33F	**Smith** Wigan	
JP 6687	AEC Regal I	C33F	**Smith** Wigan	
JP 6688	AEC Regal I	C33F	**Smith** Wigan	
JP 7122	Leyland Tiger PS1/1	C33F	**Smith** Wigan	*rebodied by Harrington FC33F in 1953*
JP 7168	Leyland Tiger PS1/1	C33F	**Smith** Wigan	
WJ 7176	Leyland Tiger TS4	® C33F	**Walker** Liverpool	

®   rebodied

◖◗ photograph on opposite page

JNC 4
EUJ 788

JP 6689

reg no	chassis	body layout	supplied to	
ORE 101	Leyland Tiger PS1/1	C33F	**Austin** Stafford	*rebodied with second-hand Burlingham FC33F with Boddy of Bridlington 1959*
ORF 945	Leyland Tiger PS1/1	C33F	**Austin** Stafford	
PRE 127	Leyland Tiger PS1/1	C33F	**Austin** Stafford	
PRF 291	Leyland Tiger PS1/1	C33F	**Austin** Stafford	*rebuilt and rebodied by NCME FL33/30F with Barton of Chilwell, re-registered 796 BAL in 1959*
PRF 343	Leyland Tiger PS1/1	C33F	**Austin** Stafford	
ORF 179	Leyland Tiger PS1/1	C33F	**Byrne** Leek	
MNU 564	Leyland Tiger PS1/1	C33F	**Dimbleby** Ashover	
MNU 71	Leyland Tiger PS1/1	C33F	**Glossop Carriage Co** Glossop	
RB 8165	Leyland Tiger TS4	Ⓡ C33F	**Glossop Carriage Co** Glossop	
JNE 382	Crossley SD42/3	C33F	**Hackett** Manchester	
JNE 383	Crossley SD42/3	C33F	**Hackett** Manchester	
JNE 797	Crossley SD42/3	C33F	**Hackett** Manchester	
JNF 999	Crossley SD42/3	C33F	**Hackett** Manchester	
ACP 816	Leyland Tiger PS1/1	C33F	**Holdsworth** Halifax	
ACP 817	Leyland Tiger PS1/1	C33F	**Holdsworth** Halifax	
EUJ 781	Crossley SD42/6	C33F	**Jones** Market Drayton	
EUJ 782	Crossley SD42/6	C33F	**Jones** Market Drayton	
EUJ 783	Leyland Tiger TS7	Ⓡ C33F	**Jones** Market Drayton	*original registration BWB 184*
CWH 700	AEC Regal III	C33F	**Knowles** Bolton	
FDM 80	Leyland Tiger PS1/1	C33F	**Lloyd** Bagillt	*rebodied by Duple FC37C in 1953*
TJ 7710	Leyland Tiger TS6	Ⓡ C33F	**Lloyd** Nuneaton	
HXJ 566	AEC Regal III	C33F	**Mayne** Manchester	
HXJ 567	AEC Regal III	C33F	**Mayne** Manchester	
JNC 3	AEC Regal III	C33F	**Mayne** Manchester	
JNC 4	AEC Regal III	C33F	**Mayne** Manchester	
BRN 690	Leyland Tiger PS1/1	C33F	**Scout** Preston	
EBU 816	Leyland Tiger PS1/1	C33F	**Shaw** Oldham	
JP 6689	Leyland Tiger PS1/1	C33F	**Smith** Wigan	*later fitted with full front*
JP 6967	Leyland Tiger PS1	C33F	**Smith** Wigan	
JP 7016	Leyland Tiger PS1/1	C33F	**Smith** Wigan	
JP 7177	Leyland Tiger PS1/1	C33F	**Smith** Wigan	*later rebuilt with full front by Samlesbury*
JP 7187	Leyland Tiger PS1/1	C33F	**Smith** Wigan	*rebodied by Harrington FC35F in 1953*
EBU 494	Leyland Tiger PS1/1	C33F	**Spencer** Oldham	
EBU 495	AEC Regal III	C33F	**Spencer** Oldham	
EBU 496	AEC Regal III	C33F	**Spencer** Oldham	
EBU 497	AEC Regal III	C33F	**Spencer** Oldham	
EBU 498	AEC Regal III	C33F	**Spencer** Oldham	
EBU 790	Leyland Tiger PS1/1	C33F	**Spencer** Oldham	
EBU 817	Leyland Tiger PS1/1	C33F	**Spencer** Oldham	
KMA 813	AEC Regal 4	Ⓡ C33F	**Sykes** Sale	*original registration FS 8578*
EUJ 788	Crossley SD42/6	C33F	**Vagg** Knockin Heath	
EUJ 789	Crossley SD42/6	C33F	**Vagg** Knockin Heath	
CK 4721	Leyland Tiger TS6	Ⓡ C33F	**Webster** Wigan	
CK 4748	Leyland Tiger TS6	Ⓡ C33F	**Webster** Wigan	
JC 3551	Leyland Tiger TS7	Ⓡ C33F	**Webster** Wigan	
JTD 377	Leyland Tiger PS1/1	C33F	**Woodcock** Heskin	
JNB 259	Maudslay Marathon III	C33F	**York Motors** Manchester	*later rebuilt FC35F by KW Bodies*

Ⓡ   rebodied

📷   photograph on opposite page

HUP 159

DBN 920   EN 9711

MHN 260

reg no	chassis		body type & layout	supplied to	
KPT 144	Crossley SD42/7		C35F	**Atkinson** Chester-le-Street	
EN 9710	Crossley SD42/7		C33F	**Auty** Bury	
■ EN 9711	Crossley SD42/7		C33F	**Auty** Bury	
JP 7339	Commer Q4	®	C30F	**Bibby** Wigan	
BEB 184	Crossley SD42/7		C33F	**Brown** Guyhim	
DBN 919	Austin K4/SL	Roadmaster	FC31F	**Butterworth** Blackpool	
■ DBN 920	Austin K4/SL	Roadmaster	FC31F	**Butterworth** Blackpool	*converted to forward control before bodying*
BWW 238	Dennis Lancet II	®	C35F	**Camplejohn** Darfield	*in 1951 converted to forward control and*
DDB 525	Commer Q4	®	C30F	**Cooper** Bredbury	*fitted by Beccols with a Roadmaster front becoming FC32F, still with Cooper*
DHJ 397	Commer Q4	®	C30F	**Cox** Southend	
HWU 746	Crossley SD42/7		C33F	**Den-Roy** Hebden Bridge	*body removed by Gardiner in 1950 and fitted to*
DBA 939	Crossley SD42/7		C33F	**Fieldsend** Salford	*Albion Valkyrie HUP 159, replacing ACB body ■*
JUP 861	Crossley SD42/7		C33F	**Gardiner** Low Spennymoor	*KPT 716 then fitted with new Beccols FC33F*
KPT 716	Crossley SD42/7		C33F	**Gardiner** Low Spennymoor	*- see 1950*
JTJ 490	AEC Regal	®	C33F	**Holden** Oswaldtwistle	
JOM 800	Crossley SD42/7		C33F	**Jackson** Castle Bromwich	*original registration GF 507*
KTJ 773	Crossley SD42/7		C33F	**Kynaston** Newton-le-Willows	
EUX 517	Crossley SD42/7		C33F	**Martlew & Ashley** Donnington Wood	
JTE 967	Leyland Tiger PS1/1		C33F	**Mayers** Liverpool	*later rebuilt with full front*
KTD 876	Crossley SD42/7		C33F	**Monks** Leigh	*later rebuilt with full front and new rear end*
KTD 877	Foden PVSC5		C33F	**Monks** Leigh	
GCA 28	Austin K2/VK	Roadmaster ®	FC31F	**E G Peters** Llanarmon	*ex government lorry, converted to*
FUO 958	Commer Q4	®	C30F	**Pickwick** Radcliffe	*forward control before bodying*
BTF 135	Leyland Tiger TS7	®	C33F	**Progress** Chorley	
WH 5804	Leyland Tiger TS6	®	C33F	**Shaw** Bolton	
GVJ 86	Bedford Special		C29F	**Sheppard** Broad Town Swindon	*chassis assembled from spares by Praill of Hereford*
JP 7865	AEC Regal III	Roadmaster	FC31F	**Smith** Wigan	
JP 7866	AEC Regal III	Roadmaster	FC15F	**Smith** Wigan	*soon altered to 31 seats*
JP 8050	Leyland Tiger PS2/3	Roadmaster	FC31F	**Smith** Wigan	
JP 8051	Leyland Tiger PS2/3	Roadmaster	FC31F	**Smith** Wigan	
EVA 409	Commer Q4	®	C30F	**Stokes** Carstairs	
EVA 410	Commer Q4	®	C30F	**Stokes** Carstairs	
EVA 411	Commer Q4	®	C30F	**Stokes** Carstairs	
HWY 363	Crossley SD42/7		C33F	**Thompson** Swinefleet	
LHN 1	Crossley SD42/7		C33F	**Voy** Darlington	
■ MHN 260	Maudslay Marathon III		C33F	**Voy** Darlington	
ENJ 602	Commer Q4	®	C30F	**Warren** Tenterden	
LCV 203	Commer Q4	®	C30F	**Weston** East Looe	
GFY 716	Morris Commercial OP/R	Roadmaster	C32F	**Whiteside** Blackpool	*built for the associated Howard fleet, not used until June 1950*
EVA 787	Commer Q4	®	C30F	**Whiteford** Lanark	

® rebodied

■ photograph on opposite page

ⓡ	rebodied		
◨	photograph below		
◨	photograph on page 101		

reg no	chassis		body type & layout	supplied to
EN 9535	Crossley SD42/6		C33F	**Auty** Bury
EN 9536	Crossley SD42/7		C33F	**Auty** Bury
SRE 941	Foden PVSC6		C33F	**Bassett** Tittensor
LMA 232	Crossley SD42/7		C33F	**Brazendale** Sale
BWA 410	Leyland Titan TD4	ⓡ	C33F	**Cash** Urmston
BU 7946	Leyland Titan TD3	ⓡ	C33F	**Dimbleby** Ashover
JO 8452	AEC Regent	ⓡ	C33F	**Dransfield** Buxton
KTC 864	Crossley SD42/7		C33F	**Eaves** Ashton-in-Makerfield
DDB 955	Crossley SD42/7		C33F	**Edwards** Marple
LMA 112	Guy Arab III 6DC		C33F	**Fairclough** Ingleton
EUX 600	Crossley SD42/7		C33F	**Hampson** Oswestry
FAW 601	Crossley SD42/7		C33F	**Hampson** Oswestry
BWB 88	Leyland Tiger TS7	ⓡ	C33F	**Hart** Coppull
FBU 181	Crossley SD42/7		C33F	**Healing** Oldham
FBU 182	Crossley SD42/7		C33F	**Healing** Oldham
FBU 183	Crossley SD42/7		C33F	**Healing** Oldham
FBU 184	Crossley SD42/7		C33F	**Healing** Oldham
FBU 185	Crossley SD42/7		C33F	**Healing** Oldham
FBU 186	Crossley SD42/7		C33F	**Healing** Oldham
FBU 187	Crossley SD42/7		C33F	**Healing** Oldham
FBU 188	Crossley SD42/7		C33F	**Healing** Oldham
FBU 189	Crossley SD42/7		C33F	**Healing** Oldham

fitted with full front in 1952 probably by Lawton of Kidsgrove

fitted with full front by Santus in 1952

fitted with Bellhouse Hartwell Monarch full front in 1952

GCA 54

JO 8452

reg no	chassis		body type & layout	**supplied to**	
KTF 446	Crossley SD42/7		C33F	**Hoyle** Haslingden	
KTF 447	Crossley SD42/7		C33F	**Hoyle** Haslingden	
FNT 40	Crossley SD42/7		C33F	**Jones** Market Drayton	
FUN 172	Crossley SD42/7		C33F	**Jones** Ruabon	
GCA 54	Foden PVSC6		C33F	**Jones** Ruabon	
KTD 623	Crossley SD42/7		C33F	**Lamb** Appley Bridge	
LLG 590	Crossley SD42/7		C33F	**Lingley** Stretford	
LLG 591	Crossley SD42/7		C33F	**Lingley** Stretford	
JP 7537	Crossley SD42/7		C33F	**Liptrot** Platt Bridge	rebodied Duple FC35F in 1955
JP 7538	Crossley SD42/7		C33F	**Liptrot** Platt Bridge	fitted with full front by Lawton in 1954
FDM 570	Crossley SD42/7		C33F	**Lloyd** Bagillt	later fitted with full front
FDM 571	Foden PVSC6		C35F	**Lloyd** Bagillt	
FDM 572	AEC Regal III		C35F	**Lloyd** Bagillt	
PRF 862	Leyland Tiger PS1/1		C35F	**Mainwaring** Bignall End	
RRE 453	Leyland Tiger PS1/1		C35F	**Mainwaring** Bignall End	
DDB 684	Crossley SD42/6		C33F	**Melba** Reddish	
DDB 763	Crossley SD42/7		C33F	**Melba** Reddish	
JOP 414	Foden PVSC6		C33F	**Myatt** Birmingham	
JM 8905	Leyland Comet CPO1		C33F	**Robinson** Appleby	
EUX 908	Tilling Stevens K6MA7		C33F	**Salopia** Whitchurch	later rebuilt to FC35F by Lawton in 1958 with Bassett of Tittensor
EUX 909	Foden PVSC6		C33F	**Salopia** Whitchurch	
FAW 771	Crossley SD42/7		C35F	**Salopia** Whitchurch	
HWU 512	Crossley SD42/6		C33F	**Scott** Mytholmroyd	
VH 9201	AEC Regent	®	C33F	**Shaw** Oldham	
EBU 961	Leyland Tiger PS1/1		C33F	**Shearing** Oldham	rebuilt to full front when with Smith of Darfield
FBU 235	Foden PVSC6		C33F	**Shearing** Oldham	
FBU 297	Guy Arab III 6DC		C33F	**Shearing** Oldham	
EUX 599	Crossley SD42/7		C33F	**Smith** Trench	
FAW 758	Crossley SD42/7		C33F	**Smith** Trench	
JP 1570	Leyland Tiger TS7	®	C33F	**Smith** Wigan	
JP 7692	Leyland Tiger PS1/1		C33F	**Smith** Wigan	
JP 7839	AEC Regal III		C33F	**Smith** Wigan	rebodied with ex-Ribble Duple C31F with Blankley of Colsterworth in 1959
JP 7852	AEC Regal III		C33F	**Smith** Wigan	
JP 7884	AEC Regal III		FC31F	**Smith** Wigan	
JP 7962	AEC Regal III		FC31F	**Smith** Wigan	
JP 8033	Crossley SD42/7		FC31F	**Smith** Wigan	
FBU 307	Leyland Tiger PS1/1		C33F	**Spencer** Oldham	
JP 7611	Crossley SD42/7		C33F	**Stringfellow** Wigan	
JP 7612	Crossley SD42/7		C33F	**Stringfellow** Wigan	
KKC 41	Foden PVSC6		C33F	**Topping** Liverpool	
FAW 786	Guy Arab III 6DC		C33F	**Vagg** Knockin Heath	
FAW 787	Guy Arab III 6DC		C33F	**Vagg** Knockin Heath	
KTE 340	Crossley SD42/7		C33F	**Warburton** Bury	
HWU 482	Crossley SD42/6		C33F	**Wood** Mirfield	later rebuilt with Burlingham Seagull full front
CWB 468	Leyland Titan TD4	®	C33F	**Woodcock** Heskin	
DCT 696	Crossley SD42/6		C33F	**Wootton** Deeping St James	
CMC 269	AEC Regent	®	C33F	**Wright** Bootle	
CWA 496	AEC Regent	®	C35F	**Wright** Bootle	
EM 4501	AEC LMT rebuild	®	C35F	**Wright** Bootle	
VH 5730	AEC Regent	®	C33F	**Wright** Bootle	
KVO 127	AEC Regal III		C35F	**Wright** Newark	

® rebodied

◧ photograph on opposite page

◧ photograph on next page

EBU 961

KTD 623

Surplus bodies

Some of the 1947, 1948 and 1949 Beccols and Bellhouse Hartwell bodies that were surplus when their owners replaced them with new, more up to date, full-front bodies in 1952, 1953 and 1954, were removed and re-used on other, older chassis. Where known, these are noted in the lists. The principal source was Smith's of Wigan which modernised several chassis by fitting them with new Harrington full-front bodies and selling the Bellhouse Hartwell and Beccols bodies.

One such Bellhouse Hartwell body was fitted to LMT 82, a much-travelled Leyland TS7 that started life in 1936 as HB 5073 of John of Hirwaun, was taken by the War Department and later ran for various London operators. KW Bodies of Blackpool bought it in 1953 and fitted a body originally on a Smith's vehicle.

In 1953 Benson of Accrington fitted Leyland TD3 TJ 6999 with a second-hand Bellhouse Hartwell body; also in 1953 Leyland TS8 JP 3055 with Knowles of Leigh was fitted with a late 1948/1949-style second-hand Beccols body.

Leyland TS7 DNA 591 was fitted with the Beccols body from JP 6468 in 1953 when with Moore of Great Witley.

JP 3055

DNA 591

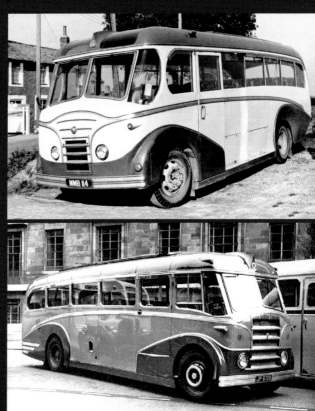

LYL 721 | MMB 114
WHL 788 | JP 6138
LAL 927

reg no	chassis	body type & layout		supplied to	
LUP 442	Crossley SD42/9C	Roadmaster	FC35F	**Atkinson** Chester-le-Street	
KVF 246	AEC Regal III	Roadmaster	FC33F	**Babbage** Cromer	
LKD 105	Crossley SD42/9A	Roadmaster	FC37F	**Baker** Aintree	
LAL 849	Leyland Comet CPO1	Roadmaster	FC32F	**Barton** Chilwell no.620	
LNN 802	Barton BTS1	Roadmaster ®	FC43F	**Barton** Chilwell no.631	see note below
LNN 886	Leyland Tiger PS2/3	Roadmaster	FC43F	**Barton** Chilwell no.630	
LRR 691	Barton BTS1	Roadmaster ®	FC43F	**Barton** Chilwell no.632	
EF 9344	AEC Regal III	Roadmaster	FC25F	**Bee-Line** West Hartlepool	rebodied Yeates FC35F when with Ribblesdale, Blackburn, 1953
EF 9369	AEC Regal III	Roadmaster	FC25F	**Bee-Line** West Hartlepool	altered to 30 seat and registered LYL 721 after tour of USA and Canada
(LYL 721)	Leyland Royal Tiger PSU1/15		C36F	**Blue Cars** London	
MMN 38	Commer Q4	®	C30F	**Clague** Douglas	intended for Altrincham Coachways, allocated registration LLG 327 cancelled
MMN 85	Albion Victor FT3AB	Roadmaster	C32F	**Collister** Douglas	
(JWW 676)	Crossley SD42/7	Roadmaster	FC33F	*Crossley Motors demonstrator*	sold to Thompson of Swinefleet in 1950 and registered as shown
LTD 972	AEC Regal III	Roadmaster	FC33F	**Felstead & White** Newton-le-Willows	
KPT 716	Crossley SD42/7	Roadmaster ®	FC33F	**Gardiner** Low Spennymoor	new body, previous Beccols C33F removed and fitted to Gardiner's Albion Valkyrie HUP 159 see note in 1949 list
LPT 3	AEC Regal III	Roadmaster	FC33F	**Gardiner** Low Spennymoor	
KUF 15	Morris Commercial PP/R	Roadmaster	C32F	**Hart** Brighton	
LMN 873	Leyland Comet CPO1		C33F	**Kneen** Douglas	re-registered WHL 788, 1962 with King, Bradford
MMB 114	Commer Avenger	Roadmaster	C33F	**Naylor** Stockton Heath	
DBU 425	Leyland Tiger PS1/1	Roadmaster ®	FC33F	**Parker** Hollinwood	
FRT 662	Commer Q4	®	C34F	**Pickwick** Radcliffe	
LTC 786	Leyland Tiger PS1/1	Roadmaster	FC35F	**Progress** Chorley	
LTF 931	Leyland Tiger PS1/1	Roadmaster	FC35F	**Progress** Chorley	
LTJ 736	Crossley SD42/7	Roadmaster	FC33F	**Progress** Chorley	
JP 8145	AEC Regal III	Roadmaster	FC31F	**Smith** Wigan	
JP 8146	AEC Regal III	Roadmaster	FC31F	**Smith** Wigan	
JP 8147	AEC Regal III	Roadmaster	FC25F	**Smith** Wigan	soon altered to 31 seats
JP 8148	AEC Regal III	Roadmaster	FC31F	**Smith** Wigan	
JP 8149	AEC Regal III	Roadmaster	FC31F	**Smith** Wigan	
JP 8150	AEC Regal III	Roadmaster	FC31F	**Smith** Wigan	
FBU 886	Leyland Tiger PS2/3	Roadmaster	FC33F	**Stretford Motors** Hollinwood	
FBU 887	Leyland Tiger PS1/1	Roadmaster	FC33F	**Stretford Motors** Hollinwood	
GPY 17	Leyland Tiger PS2/3	Roadmaster	FC37F	**Sunter** Northallerton	
LTF 996	Leyland Tiger PS1/1	Roadmaster	FC33F	**Taylor** Earlestown	rebodied Plaxton FC35F in 1958 with Peascod, Liverpool
LAL 927	AEC Regal III	Roadmaster	FC33F	**Wright** Newark	

major rebuild

reg no	chassis	body type & layout		supplied to	
JP 6138	Leyland Tiger PS1/1		FC33F	**Stringfellow** Wigan	Roadmaster front fitted to original Santus body

LAL 849
chassis rebuilt to forward control before rebodying

LNN 802 LRR 691
chassis built from pairs of pre-war Leyland TD
HG 2305, JY 6730 & HG 2715, JY 9423

LNN 886
chassis lengthened to 30ft before bodying

® rebodied

◧ photograph on opposite page

HF 9175   JWD 284
JP 8143   NLG 586
TJ 7525   LDV 640
           MFM 31

reg no	chassis	body type & layout			supplied to	
■ HF 9175	Leyland Titan TD3		®	C33F	**Andrew** Tideswell	
KYF 894	Foden PVSC6			FC33F	**Ansell** London	
LLW 434	Foden PVFE6	**Atlantic**		FC39C	**Ansell** London	
FNV 541	Albion Valiant CX39N			C33F	**Basford** Greens Norton	
KDF 331	Fordson ET6	SHORT		C29F	**Beavis** Bussage	
■ (JP 8143)	Foden PVFE6	**Atlantic**		FC39C	*demonstrator*	sold to Smith of Wigan in 1950, registered as shown
(EFR 627)	Fordson ET6	SHORT		C30F	*demonstrator*	sold to Slack of Blackpool in 1950, registered as shown
JWU 117	Leyland Tiger PS1/1			C33F	**Central** Ripponden	
GAW 407	Leyland Comet CPO1			C33F	**Corvedale** Ludlow	
GAW 636	AEC Regal III			C33F	**Corvedale** Ludlow	
■ TJ 7525	Leyland Titan TD3		®	C33F	**Dimbleby** Ashover	
ASD 232	Bedford OWB		®	C29F	**Dodds** Troon	uncertain whether rebodied for McAteer of Dumbarton or Dodds
FDR 54	Tilling Stevens K6LA7			FC33F	**Embankment** Plymouth	
RPU 509	Fordson ET6	LONG		RC34F	**Ford Motor Co** Dagenham	
KRH 905	Leyland Tiger PS1/1			C35F	**Frostways** Hull	
PS 2038	Fordson ET6	SHORT		C29F	**Ganson** Lerwick	
NHA 392	Albion Valiant CX39N			FC33F	**Gilbert & Houghton** Smethwick	
FBU 190	Crossley SD42/7			C33F	**Healing** Oldham	
LTD 787	Leyland Comet CPO1			C33F	**Ireland** Lancaster	
NBH 150	Leyland Comet ECPO1R			C22F	**Jeffways** High Wycombe	
JUE 479	Leyland Tiger PS1/1			C35F	**Lloyd** Nuneaton	
JUE 913	Leyland Tiger PS1/1			C35F	**Lloyd** Nuneaton	
JWD 136	Foden PVSC6			C35F	**Lloyd** Nuneaton	
■ JWD 284	Leyland Tiger PS1/1			C35F	**Lloyd** Nuneaton	
EDB 14	Foden PVFE6	**Atlantic**		FC39C	**Melba** Reddish	
GVJ 785	Leyland Tiger PS1/1			C33F	**Morgan** Hereford	
GVJ 786	Leyland Tiger PS1/1			C33F	**Morgan** Hereford	
NAF 509	Tilling Stevens K6MA7	**Monarch**		FC33F	**Newquay Motor Co** Newquay	
■ NLG 586	Fordson ET6	SHORT		C30F	**Parkside Hospital** Macclesfield	
JWK 95	Albion Valiant CX39N			C33F	**Partridge** Coventry	rebuilt with full front 1952
LTF 28	AEC Regal III			FC33F	**Pearson** Heywood	
LTD 536	Foden PVSC6			FC33F	**Rigby** Patricroft	
GBU 179	Foden PVFE6	**Atlantic**		FC39C	**Shaw** Oldham	
GBU 180	Foden PVFE6	**Atlantic**		FC39C	**Shaw** Oldham	
JP 1689	Leyland Tiger TS7		®	C33F	**Smith** Wigan	
JP 7885	AEC Regal III			FC31F	**Smith** Wigan	
JP 8075	Leyland Tiger PS2/3			FC31F	**Smith** Wigan	
JP 8076	Leyland Tiger PS1/1			FC31F	**Smith** Wigan	
JP 8631	Foden PVFE6	**Atlantic**		FC39C	**Smith** Wigan	
JP 8632	Foden PVFE6	**Atlantic**		FC39C	**Smith** Wigan	
JP 8633	Foden PVRF6	**Landmaster I**		C41C	**Smith** Wigan	prototype Landmaster, demonstrated at the 1950 Commercial Motor Show with 41 seats, altered to 39 after the show
JP 2294	Leyland Tiger TS7		®	C33F	**Stringfellow** Wigan	
JP 8158	Crossley SD42/7			FC33F	**Stringfellow** Wigan	
■ LDV 640	Leyland Comet CPO1			C33F	**Sunbeam** Torquay	
ORB 952	Foden PVFE6	**Atlantic**		FC39C	**Swain** Somercotes	
■ MFM 31	Foden PVSC6			FC37F	**Taylor** Chester	
LTJ 904	Foden PVFE6	**Atlantic**		FC39C	**Taylor** Leigh	
LKA 718	Foden PVFE6	**Atlantic**		FC39C	**Topping** Liverpool	
LKB 525	Commer Avenger			C33F	**Topping** Liverpool	
TF 6334	Leyland Tiger TS1		®	C35F	**Turner** Chorley	
ARA 887	Leyland Tiger TS6		®	C33F	**Woodcock** Heskin	

® rebodied

■ photograph on opposite page

LYL 725
PHA 298

reg no	chassis	body type & layout		supplied to	
GDM 682	Tilling Stevens K6LA7	Roadmaster	FC33F	**Bellis** Buckley	
GET 601	Leyland Royal Tiger PSU1/15		C41C	**Billies** Mexborough	
LYL 722	Leyland Royal Tiger PSU1/15		C30F	**Blue Cars** London	
LYL 723	Leyland Royal Tiger PSU1/15		C30F	**Blue Cars** London	
LYL 724	Leyland Royal Tiger PSU1/15		C30F	**Blue Cars** London	
LYL 725	Leyland Royal Tiger PSU1/15		C30F	**Blue Cars** London	
LYL 726	Leyland Royal Tiger PSU1/15		C30F	**Blue Cars** London	
EWH 417	Austin K4/CXD	Roadmaster	C33F	**Butterworth** Blackpool	
NTC 611	AEC Regal III	Roadmaster	FC35F	**Florence** Morecambe	rebodied by Plaxton FC35F in 1953
NTC 610	AEC Regal III	Roadmaster	FC35F	**Kia-Ora** Morecambe	
NTF 328	Karrier Q25		C14F	**Makinson** Blackburn	
BWX 331	Leyland Lion LT7	Roadmaster ℝ	FC33F	**Mann** Smethwick	
PHA 298	Leyland Tiger TS6	Roadmaster ℝ	FC33F	**Mann** Smethwick	original registration thought to be CK 4738
MTF 298	Leyland Royal Tiger PSU1/11		C41C	**Monks** Leigh	
MTE 550	Leyland Royal Tiger PSU1/11		C41C	**Progress** Chorley	
NTB 147	Leyland Titan TD5	Roadmaster ℝ	FC37F	**Sharrock** Westhoughton	original registration not traced
GET 707	Leyland Royal Tiger PSU1/15		C39C	**Smart** Greasborough	
MTE 837	Leyland Royal Tiger PSU1/11		C41C	**Taylor** Earlestown	
MKA 741	AEC Regal III	Roadmaster	FC37F	**Walker** Liverpool	
MRR 295	AEC Regal IV		C41C	**Wright** Newark	

rebuilds

reg no	chassis	body type & layout		supplied to	
KOE 201	Morris Commercial OP/R		C21F	**Blue Cars** London	
KOE 202	Morris Commercial OP/R		C21F	**Blue Cars** London	
KOE 203	Morris Commercial OP/R		C21F	**Blue Cars** London	
KOE 204	Morris Commercial OP/R		C21F	**Blue Cars** London	
KOE 205	Morris Commercial OP/R		C21F	**Blue Cars** London	Roadmaster front end
KOE 206	Morris Commercial OP/R		C21F	**Blue Cars** London	rebuild of Plaxton body new in 1950
KOE 207	Morris Commercial OP/R		C21F	**Blue Cars** London	
KOE 208	Morris Commercial OP/R		C21F	**Blue Cars** London	
KOE 209	Morris Commercial OP/R		C21F	**Blue Cars** London	
KOE 210	Morris Commercial OP/R		C21F	**Blue Cars** London	
KOE 211	Morris Commercial OP/R		C21F	**Blue Cars** London	
KOE 212	Morris Commercial OP/R		C21F	**Blue Cars** London	
PVX 363	Morris Commercial OP/R		C21F	**Blue Cars** London	Roadmaster front end rebuild of Page body new in 1950
DDB 525	Commer Q4		FC32F	**Cooper** Bredbury	rebuilt to forward control with Roadmaster front - see DDB 525 in 1949 list

ℝ   rebodied

📷   photograph on opposite page

DRN 928

LOJ 77 | VMX 256

reg no	chassis	body type & layout		supplied to	
NYB 191	AEC Regal IV	**Landmaster II**	C35C	**Berry** Bradford-on-Tone	
TEV 910	Fordson ET6	SHORT	C30F	**Brentwood Mental Hospital**	
LOL 993	Fordson ET6	SHORT	C30F	**Butlin** Birmingham	
VMX 256	Fordson ET6	SHORT	C30F	**Chambers** Uxbridge	
GBU 877	Leyland Tiger TS8	**Monarch** Ⓡ	FC35F	**Dyson** Hollinwood	original registration AAG 118
JSP 850	Fordson ET7	LONG	C34F	**Fleming** Anstruther	
PHA 357	Albion Viking HD61	**Monarch**	C35F	**Gilbert & Houghton** Smethwick	
OLG 728	Guy Arab III 6DC	**Monarch**	FC35F	**Gleave** Nantwich	
MTJ 426	Leyland Tiger PS2/3	**Monarch**	FC37F	**Gregson** Skelmersdale	rebodied by Plaxton FC37F in 1960
NTC 445	Leyland Royal Tiger PSU1/11	**Landmaster II**	C41C	**Hart** Coppull	
NBH 910	Maudslay Marathon III	**Monarch**	FC33F	**Jeffways** High Wycombe	
EWH 168	AEC Regal IV	**Landmaster II**	C41C	**Knowles** Bolton	
EWH 169	AEC Regal IV	**Landmaster II**	C41C	**Knowles** Bolton	
LOE 999	Fordson ET6	SHORT	C30F	**Langho Colony (hospital)** Blackburn	
EJA 367	Foden PVRF6	**Landmaster I**	C43C	**Melba** Reddish	
HCA 650	AEC Regal IV	**Landmaster II**	C41C	**(Meredith &) Jesson** Cefn Mawr	
NRL 61	Tilling Stevens K6MA7	**Monarch**	FC33F	**Newquay Motor Co** Newquay	
HDM 196	Foden PVRF6	**Landmaster I**	C41C	**Phillips & Hodgkinson** Bagillt	
LOE 701	Fordson ET6	LONG	C30F	**Reeve** Rubery	long wheelbase but only 30 seats
LOE 702	Fordson ET6	LONG	C30F	**Reeve** Rubery	
GBU 647	Leyland Tiger PS1/1	**Monarch**	FC35F	**Renton** Hollinwood	
GBU 729	Leyland Royal Tiger PSU1/15	**Landmaster II**	C41C	**Renton** Hollinwood	
KWT 978	Leyland Royal Tiger PSU1/15	**Landmaster II**	C41C	**Ripponden & District** Ripponden	
DRN 363	Leyland Royal Tiger PSU1/15	**Landmaster II**	C41C	**Scout** Preston	
DRN 926	Leyland Royal Tiger PSU1/15	**Landmaster II**	C41C	**Scout** Preston	
DRN 927	Leyland Royal Tiger PSU1/15	**Landmaster II**	C41C	**Scout** Preston	
DRN 928	Leyland Royal Tiger PSU1/15	**Landmaster II**	C41C	**Scout** Preston	
DRN 929	Leyland Royal Tiger PSU1/15	**Landmaster II**	C41C	**Scout** Preston	
DRN 930	Leyland Royal Tiger PSU1/11	**Landmaster II**	C41C	**Scout** Preston	
NTC 354	Guy Arab III 6DC	**Monarch**	FC35F	**Smith** St Helens	
JP 6158	Leyland Tiger PS1/1	**Monarch** Ⓡ	FC33F	**Stringfellow** Wigan	
MTJ 29	Foden PVRF6	**Landmaster I**	C41C	**Taylor** Leigh	
LOH 856	Foden PVRG6	**Landmaster I**	C32C	**Transglobe** Birmingham	
LOJ 77	AEC Regal IV	**Landmaster II**	C32C	**Transglobe** Birmingham	
DSD 583	Foden PVRF6	**Landmaster I**	C41C	**West of Scotland** Ayr	
BHF 30	Austin K4/CXD	**Monarch**	C32F	**Wilkinson** Wallasey	

Ⓡ rebodied

◼ photograph on opposite page

MOC 707 | OTB 644
NTJ 770

reg no	chassis	body type & layout			supplied to	
OTB 861	Leyland Tiger TS7	Roadmaster	®	FC33F	**Sharrock** Westhoughton	
RHA 792	AEC Regal	Monarch	®	FC37F	**Ashmore** Smethwick	original registration CFC 782 chassis lengthened to 30ft
MLF 341	Leyland Royal Tiger PSU1/15	Landmaster III		C32C	**Blue Cars** London	
MLF 342	Leyland Royal Tiger PSU1/15	Landmaster III		C32C	**Blue Cars** London	
MLF 343	Leyland Royal Tiger PSU1/15	Landmaster III		C32C	**Blue Cars** London	
MLF 344	Leyland Royal Tiger PSU1/15	Landmaster III		C32C	**Blue Cars** London	
MLF 345	Leyland Royal Tiger PSU1/15	Landmaster III		C32C	**Blue Cars** London	
MLF 346	Leyland Royal Tiger PSU1/15	Landmaster III		C32C	**Blue Cars** London	
MXV 347	Leyland Royal Tiger PSU1/15	Landmaster III		C32C	**Blue Cars** London	
MXV 348	Leyland Royal Tiger PSU1/15	Landmaster III		C32C	**Blue Cars** London	cancelled chassis order for Brazilian operator 33ft long, lefthand drive
MXV 440	Leyland Royal Tiger LOPSU1/1	Landmaster III		C32C	**Blue Cars** London	
MYV 637	Sentinel SLC6	Landmaster IV		C32C	**Blue Cars** London	cancelled order for Drake Tours for use in Argentina; 33ft long, lefthand drive
JYS 136	Fordson ET6	SHORT		C29F	**Dept of Health for Scotland** Glasgow	
OHW 407	Fordson ET6	SHORT		C32F	**Devon Mental Hospital** Exminster	
EDR 507	Maudslay Marathon III	Monarch	®	FC33F	**Embankment** Plymouth	
EDR 727	Maudslay Marathon III	Monarch	®	FC33F	**Embankment** Plymouth	
LMU 605	Fordson ET6	LONG		C29F	**Friern Mental Hospital** London	
◧ OTB 644	AEC Regal IV	Landmaster III		C41C	**Mills & Seddon** Farnworth	
◧ NTJ 770	Leyland Royal Tiger PSU1/15	Landmaster III		C41C	**Monks** Leigh	rebodied Plaxton C43F when with Walton Hall Garage of Liverpool 1965
JP 5760	Leyland Tiger PS1/1	Monarch	®	FC35F	**Morris & Stringfellow** Wigan	
ORL 518	AEC Regal IV	Landmaster II		C41C	**Newquay Motor Co** Newquay	
ORL 519	AEC Regal IV	Landmaster II		C41C	**Newquay Motor Co** Newquay	
NKA 849	Leyland Royal Tiger PSU1/15	Landmaster II		C41C	**Peascod** Liverpool	rebodied by Plaxton C41F in 1961
JP 7221	Leyland Tiger PS1/1	see note below	®	FC33F	**Smith** Wigan	
◧ MOC 707	Foden PVRG6	Landmaster II		C41C	**Smith's Imperial** Birmingham	
MOC 777	Foden PVRG6	Landmaster II		C41C	**Smith's Imperial** Birmingham	
MUB 437	AEC Regal III	Monarch	®	FC35F	**Wallace Arnold** Leeds	new body 8ft wide
MUB 438	AEC Regal III	Monarch	®	FC35F	**Wallace Arnold** Leeds	

JP 7221 had a Landmaster style body

®   rebodied

◧   photograph on opposite page

NLR 848

| TWJ 254 |
| MKV 202 | PGK 473

reg no	chassis	body type & layout		supplied to
NLR 711	Daimler Freeline D650HS	**Landmaster IV**	C32C	**Blue Cars** London
NLR 712	Daimler Freeline D650HS	**Landmaster IV**	C32C	**Blue Cars** London
NLR 713	Daimler Freeline D650HS	**Landmaster IV**	C32C	**Blue Cars** London
NLR 714	Daimler Freeline D650HS	**Landmaster IV**	C32C	**Blue Cars** London
NLR 715	Daimler Freeline D650HS	**Landmaster IV**	C32C	**Blue Cars** London
NLR 716	Daimler Freeline D650HS	**Landmaster IV**	C32C	**Blue Cars** London
◖ NLR 848	Daimler Freeline D650HS	**Landmaster IV**	C32C	**Blue Cars** London
NLR 849	Daimler Freeline D650HS	**Landmaster IV**	C32C	**Blue Cars** London
NLR 850	Sentinel SLC6	**Landmaster IV**	C30C	**Blue Cars** London
◖ MKV 202	AEC Regal IV	**Landmaster IV**	C37C	**BTS** Coventry
MKV 203	AEC Regal IV	**Landmaster IV**	C37C	**BTS** Coventry
MKV 204	AEC Regal IV	**Landmaster IV**	C37C	**BTS** Coventry

1953

used for brake development by Lockheed, into service in 1954

1952 Commercial Motor Show exhibit in Smith of Wigan livery with 32 seats

reg no	chassis	body type & layout		supplied to
OLL 946	Leyland Tiger Cub OPSUC1/1	**Landmaster IV**	C34C	**Blue Cars** London
OLL 947	Leyland Tiger Cub OPSUC1/1	**Landmaster IV**	C34C	**Blue Cars** London
OLL 948	Leyland Tiger Cub OPSUC1/1	**Landmaster IV**	C34C	**Blue Cars** London
◖ PGK 473	Leyland Royal Tiger PSU1/16	**Landmaster IV**	C34C	**Blue Cars** London
PGK 474	Leyland Royal Tiger PSU1/16	**Landmaster IV**	C34C	**Blue Cars** London
ECP 205	Leyland Royal Tiger PSU1/16	**Landmaster IV**	C37C	**Hebble** Halifax no.71
ECP 206	Leyland Royal Tiger PSU1/16	**Landmaster IV**	C37C	**Hebble** Halifax no.72
ECP 499	Leyland Royal Tiger PSU1/16	**Landmaster IV**	C37C	**Hebble** Halifax no.73
ECP 500	Leyland Royal Tiger PSU1/16	**Landmaster IV**	C37C	**Hebble** Halifax no.74

1954

OPSUC1/1 export model modified to PSUC1/2 specification by Leyland before bodying

reg no	chassis	body type & layout		supplied to
JTE 792	Leyland Tiger PS1/1	see note below ⓡ	FC33F	**Kirkby** Harthill
TWJ 253	AEC Reliance	**Landmaster IV**	C35C	**Sheffield United** Sheffield no.253
◖ TWJ 254	AEC Reliance	**Landmaster IV**	C35C	**Sheffield United** Sheffield no.254
PYU 4	AEC Reliance	**Landmaster IV**	C30C	**Tartan Arrow Service** London

1955

PYU 4 was the only coach of haulage company Tartan Arrow. It ran on hire to Northern Roadways on its Glasgow - London service. Severely damaged in an accident after a short time in service, and in 1958 was rebuilt by Tartan Arrow as a van.

JTE 792 had a Landmaster style body

ⓡ rebodied

◖ photograph on opposite page & below

Body numbers

Bellhouse Hartwell (and probably Bellhouse Higson) coach bodies were allocated numbers in a series which appears to have run from B1 to B268, with an additional series BA1-11 used from mid 1949 to early 1950 during the firm's peak output of coaches. Together these give an apparent total of 279 post-war coaches of which we have identified the 274 listed above plus some thought to be cancellations.

Despite this seeming precision, the actual body numbers are only known for a relatively small number of bodies, some are uncertain and many are unknown; because of this we have not included them.

At the bottom of the opposite page is the plate from Landmaster MKV 202 which, by an odd act of fate, ended its life derelict in the yard of O'S Coaches of Hospital, Eire, dumped directly in front of Beccols-bodied JP 8146.

These were photographed by Clive King in September 1970.

reg no	chassis	body type & layout			supplied to
?	Austin K4/CXD	metal frame		B31D	**not traced** Nigeria
JNC 717	Leyland Tiger PS1/1	**Tryphon**	Ⓡ	FC34F	**Sharp** Longsight, Manchester

although 12 were ordered, it is not certain whether 8 or 12 Austins were built and shipped

Ⓡ rebodied

📷 photograph below

One of the Tryphon's regular duties was transporting the Manchester University rugby teams to away matches. Here it is outside the University Union building on Oxford Road on a foggy February Saturday in 1959.

JOHN KAYE

Vehicle list photographers

Atlantic	Bellhouse Hartwell archive
BWB 88	NA3T/A Hustwitt
BWB 187	J S Cockshott archive
DBN 920	NA3T/A Hustwitt
DNA 591	Roy Marshall
DRN 928	J S Cockshott archive
EBU 961	J S Cockshott archive
EN 9711	Roy Marshall
EUJ 788	Roy Marshall
GCA 54	Peter Tulloch
HUP 159	Bob Kell
HF 9175	R H G Simpson
HTC 514	Robert Grieves
JNC 4	Roy Marshall
JO 8452	Roy Marshall
JP 3055	NA3T/A Hustwitt
JP 6138	Roy Marshall
JP 6323	not traced
JP 6468	Nichols archive
JP 6686	Roy Marshall
JP 6689	J S Cockshott archive
JWD 284	NA3T/A Hustwitt
KTD 623	NA3T/A Hustwitt
LAL 927	Roy Marshall
LDV 640	J S Cockshott archive
LOJ 77	J S Cockshott archive
LYL 721	Nichols archive
LYL 725	not traced
MFM 31	Bellhouse Hartwell
MHN 260	Bob Kell
MKV 202	J S Cockshott archive
MMB 114	not traced
MOC 707	Roy Marshall
NLG 586	not traced
NLR 849	J S Cockshott archive
NTJ 770	NA3T/A Hustwitt
OTB 644	NA3T/A Hustwitt
PGK 473	J S Cockshott archive
PHA 298	NA3T/A Hustwitt
TJ 7525	not traced
TWJ 254	J S Cockshott archive
WHL 788	J S Cockshott archive
VMX 256	NA3T/A Hustwitt